A Radical Agenda

After the New Right and the Old Left

David Donnison

Rivers Oram Press
London

First published in 1991 by
Rivers Oram Press
144 Hemingford Road, London N1 1DE

Published in the USA by
Paul and Company
Post Office Box 442, Concord, MA 01742

Set in Goudy Old Style by Columns of Reading
and printed in Great Britain by T.J. Press (Padstow) Ltd, Padstow, Cornwall
Designed by Lesley Stewart

British Library Cataloguing in Publication Data
Donnison, David 1926-
    A radical agenda : after the new right and the old left.
    1. Political ideologies
    I. Title
    320.01

ISBN 1-85489-029-8
ISBN 1-85489-030-1 pbk

Write the vision, and make it plain upon tables, that he may run that readeth it. For the vision is yet for an appointed time, but at the end it shall speak, and not lie: though it may tarry, wait for it; because it will surely come.

Habakkuk, II, 2-3

Contents

Tables and figures

Acknowledgments

One cannot write a book like this one without the help of all sorts of people who provide ideas, experience, advice and encouragement – usually without knowing how important their help has been. Most important of all for me have been the people who are living with the hardships I have tried to write about; people in bleak, squalid or violent neighbourhoods who are striving, along with their neighbours, to create a better world. They taught me so much of what I have tried to say, without ever thinking of themselves as collaborators in the writing of a book.

Among those who contributed comments or advice about sections or earlier drafts of the book I particularly want to thank Michael Barratt Brown, Duncan Forrester, Joe Haines, Sean and Ruth Healy, Bill Jordan, Peter Marris, Jo Roll, Ann Rosengard, Hugh Stretton and Malcolm Wicks. Anthony Harris helped me to get the final version into shape. The Socialist Philosophy Group, Glasgow University's Centre for Housing Research and Edinburgh University's Centre for Theology and Public Issues helped too. Earlier drafts of many chapters in this book have appeared elsewhere: I list these publications at the back of the book and am grateful to their editors and publishers.

The Rowntree Charitable Trust and the Barrow and Geraldine S. Cadbury Trust gave me financial support and much patient encouragement. I am very grateful for that help. An earlier grant from the Rowntree Foundation helped me to assemble the data underlying parts of chapter 7.

Kay Carmichael, my wife, with whom I have worked over every page, has been my constant comrade in the whole enterprise.

Introduction

Why this book was written

Wherever I go in the western world I meet people who are uneasy about the course their countries are taking. Others are puzzled or irritated by these anxieties. So many good things have happened in recent years: why fuss about the bad ones?

Britain offers some of the most vivid examples of the changes that are going on and the arguments they provoke. Incomes here have risen faster than the cost of living, and income tax has been reduced. More people than ever before own their own homes, and more own shares in public companies. Many people are doing very well indeed. Five years ago Britain overtook the United States to become the world's biggest importer of champagne. The complacent purr of the BMW, the mating call of the Porsche, are heard in the land.

But Britain is chalking up records of other kinds too. Those purring BMWs pass by elderly men and women sleeping in cardboard boxes. More and more of them. There are young boys begging for money in the railway stations – and being invited to rent out their most private parts for the price of a meal and a night in a warm bed. Girls too. We may soon overtake the Turks to send more of our people to prison than any other country in the western world. In back streets and the bleaker council estates black people are being attacked and abused more often than before. The police force has been one of our main growth industries.

These are outward signs of a brutalised and increasingly unequal society. During the last ten years it has been the richer half of the British people who have gained ground. After taking account of changes in incomes, prices, taxes and national insurance contributions, the poorer half of our people are worse off

1

than they were ten years ago. Those with children have done worst of all.

The fundamental causes of these changes – all across western Europe – are the growth of new occupations demanding new skills, and the decay of the older industries which used to employ so many working class people. Britain has suffered more than other countries of the European Community from these changes: poverty has grown faster here than elsewhere. Other changes have followed – many of them political results of the divisions brought about within our society by economic changes.

Long established movements for social reform have been demoralised. They have lost their capacity to resist the attacks being made on things which they held to be sacrosanct. Decaying schools which have increasing difficulty in recruiting teachers, crumbling public housing estates, lengthening queues in the social security offices and in many of our hospitals – these are the outward signs of those assaults. Meanwhile demands for places in private schools, for private medical care and for houses in the leafier suburbs have been booming as richer people take their money and run for the private sector.

The huge increases in incomes which top managers have awarded themselves might be tolerable if that was a reward for world-beating success. But British industry continues to invest less, and less efficiently, than its competitors overseas; and Britain spends less on training its workers. Not surprisingly, its share of world markets continues to decline.

The increasing wealth of the captains of British industry owes more to their political power than to their economic achievements. This power too might be tolerable if it was wisely used. But it has not been. With vociferous support from the Conservative government which many of them funded, industrial leaders oppose the growth of workers' rights which their colleagues in other European countries take for granted. The flood of imported goods, sucked in by the demands of those who have been getting richer, cannot be earned from the exports of our own ill-led, under-capitalised and poorly trained industries. Balance of payments deficits, inflation, "stop-go" styles of economic management and rising unemployment are back. As North Sea oil peters out, as we run out of publicly owned industries and assets to sell, things are likely to get worse.

Despite its claim to be curtailing the powers of the state, our government has centralised more power, has grown more aggressive in censoring the media, and is more inclined to oppress organised workers and democratic local government than any previous peace-time British regime.

The unease I discern among many of my fellow citizens is about economic failure, about social injustice, and about the coarse moral character of an increasingly oppressive regime. I meet similar, if more muted, concerns among thoughtful people in other western countries, and they are not confined to old socialists or to members of any particular Party.

Why do we seem so incapable of bringing about humane and productive political changes? Not because the collection of Victorian bric-a-brac known as the philosophy of the "New" Right has won all the arguments. And not because the Conservative government which relied on these ideas was ever backed by solid majorities of the voters. Opinion polls throughout this decade show that most of the voters have at best been sceptical about most Conservative policies.

The reason for the Conservatives' decade of political success has been the collapse of the opposition. The industries, the social groups and the institutions on which the Labour movement was built have decayed. The movement is struggling to formulate fresh principles and priorities for reform. Many books and pamphlets from the Left start by setting out the arguments of the "New" Right, from Thomas Hobbes and Adam Smith to Milton Friedman and Keith Joseph – often doing that job more cogently and clearly than the original authors ever did for themselves. Then they demolish these ideas by showing that they do not fit the modern world at all well. After that, most of them run out of steam.

In this book I try to tackle the reformers' main task: to think out what we stand for. Happily, many other people are now trying to do the same thing. I list some of them on page 197.

How the argument is presented

The book starts by going back to basic principles. That means recovering the feelings which lead people from personal experience to political action. From seeing people and things in isolation, we move to seeing them "in the world", as part of a larger social system. Only when we learn to couple this experience with justified anger and to infuse it with hope do we become capable of changing things. Thus my arguments usually start with reality – with a glimpse of life as some people experience it – and tease out principles later.

I used to start political arguments with a full and fair statement of my opponent's point of view: then criticise and reformulate that view. But this strategy accepts from the start your opponent's choice of the agenda – the battleground. This is all right if the pair of you do indeed begin from the same fundamental assumptions and have met to argue only about the details – how best to resolve problems defined in mutually agreed ways. But the world has changed. We now dispute the agenda itself.

So I start by asserting my own questions and establishing my own agenda. To do that without ever mentioning alternative points of view, however, would be a rather flabby way of proceeding. To define your own standpoint sharply it is essential to show what it excludes or denies as well as the things it affirms. I have tried to do this at regular intervals, but only after the agenda – the battleground – has been made clear, towards the end of each stage in my own argument.

Since this is essentially a democratic and egalitarian book I have tried to use words which everyone can understand. The same principle governs my use of scholarly references. To compel the reader to fight his way through a swarm of footnotes about other authors who have said much the same things would be no more than a claim to scholarly credentials. (Look how many books I've read!) So I only quote other people's work when it seems essential to do so. I list these sources more exactly and suggest further reading, chapter by chapter, in notes which will be found at the back of the book. To help readers take the discussion further I conclude each chapter with half a dozen questions that may encourage them to improve the arguments which I have so briefly launched.

How the book is organised

Chapter 1 goes back to first principles, introducing in a simple way most of the ideas and words which I shall use later on. Then I do the same thing on a larger scale in chapter 2, which discusses poverty, its meaning and significance. Chapter 3 asks: By what authority does anyone tell others how their society should be run? My answer presents the fundamental principles on which the whole book is founded. These are applied, in chapter 4, to one large issue now much discussed — the idea of human rights. Chapter 5, concluding this part of the book, draws the argument together as briefly and clearly as possible.

What difference would these principles make to policy and practice in a country like Britain? That is the question explored in Part 2 of the book which shows where my arguments would lead in practical terms. Since a discussion of this kind has to be rooted in one society, I have focussed upon the country I know best; but I hope readers from other countries can interpret Part 2 for their own purposes.

People often apply their political principles by taking one sector of the economy after another — writing first, a chapter on economic policy, then one on the environment, another on the health service, and so on. But that treatment encourages readers to assume that economic policy has to be sorted out before they can think about social policy; that health depends on doctors and health services; that housing conditions depend on housing authorities; and that everything has to wait on central government and nothing can be done till you win a majority in Parliament. None of which is true.

I have therefore sliced the issues up in a different way, taking people and the small neighbourhoods in which most of them live first of all, in chapter 6. That is the scale of action which we all understand best. It also demonstrates that many things are already being done at this level without waiting on governments.

Chapter 7 deals with action on the larger scale of a city and the region surrounding it. Places matter. Each is different. And it is people and their civic leaders who make them so. That sort of leadership is more important than we have allowed for.

Chapter 8 turns to the national scale of action, inevitably touching more briefly on the wider range of issues which have to be considered at this level. I have outlined a strategy with broad priorities, and not attempted to provide a detailed manifesto.

Chapter 9 is the only one in the book which does focus on a particular sector of the economy: housing, chosen because this is an arena which calls for private, public and voluntary initiatives, operating at all three of the scales of action examined in previous chapters. It provides, within one field, a case study of the ways in which the whole argument should work.

That leads, in Chapter 10, to conclusions brought together from all the previous chapters. If you want a summary of the philosophy and political priorities offered by this book, this is where to find it.

And that might have been the end. But many people who are convinced by most of what I say will nevertheless wonder: "So what? Does anyone bother about such things any more?" I have tried to confront that bleak question in a final chapter which explains how political change comes about, and what parts we each play in the process.

In a society as unequal and as unfair as ours, social conflicts will erupt from time to time in ways we cannot foresee, producing turbulence which discredits the ruling regime. But turbulence, by itself, only provides an opportunity for change. What use a society makes of these opportunities depends on what has been done in previous generations by people who thought and planned, tried things out, and spread the news about ideas which seemed to work.

Time is not on anyone's side. It's neutral. If good people do not furnish their society with a bank of humane, tested, reforming ideas to draw on in times of crisis, then bad people with brutal ideas will take over instead.

Part 1
Political principles

1 | Seeing, saying and doing

Believing is seeing

You are standing in a run-down street somewhere in the inner parts of a big, old city.

A man is walking towards you. He is middle-aged and wears a dirty old coat. His shoes are down at heel, his trousers are baggy, with turn-ups which are beginning to fray, and he carries in his hand a bulging plastic bag. You suspect that it contains all that he has. There is a heavy object in the pocket of his coat and you guess that it's a bottle. He walks as if he has nowhere to get to, pausing at the litter bins attached to lamp posts and sifting through them with a practised hand. He is looking – you guess – for cigarette ends.

What do you call this man? How do you describe what you are seeing?

A dosser? Drifter? Vagrant? Bum? Wino? Tramp?

These are the words which many people use. Others might call him a homeless man. Each word is heavily loaded with implications about the character and circumstances of the person they describe. They suggest that he has problems about drink, or may have spent time in prisons or mental hospitals. They also imply that he has no roots in this city – and therefore no claims on its citizens. He does not have a job or a home or a family here, is not a local tax payer, is not on the register of voters; and he'll soon move on.

The words also suggest the nature of the problem presented by this man, and the directions in which we should look for solutions. For a start, they suggest that, unlike most of the other people in the street, he has – and is – a problem of some sort. He may have needs too; but not of a kind that should be met in the

9

street where I live or in the waiting rooms of the services which I and my family use.

He will not be a problem for the building societies or the banks (he can't afford to use them) or for the mainstream services of the housing department (he could not cope with a council flat, would only upset the neighbours and endanger himself – and anyway, he'll drift away to another town soon). He will not be a problem for the home help service or the social workers who visit people in their homes (he hasn't got a home). In some towns he's not even allowed to be a problem for the ordinary social security office: they set up a special office for the "NFA cases" – the people who have no fixed abode. If he's a problem for the health services it will be the casualty wards of the hospitals, not the local GP's surgery, that will take care of him.

All of this is implied by the kinds of words we use to describe this man. They suggest that he needs special services – night shelters, hostels, detoxification units, resettlement units and the like.

The specially trained people who run these services often do so in ways which reflect their assumptions about the life styles of their customers – and reinforce those patterns. Men are sent out of hostels at ten in the morning, and told they may be allowed back in the evening if they queue outside at opening time. But they won't get the same room or the same bed as they had the night before; and if they get a room to themselves they probably won't be allowed a key for it.

Thus a self-fulfilling prophecy is fashioned. Could you keep yourself or your clothes clean when leading such a life? And when no ordinary citizen welcomes you, would it not be natural to join a bottle gang of your own mates to find the comradeship which might see you through a wet winter's day? These patterns, in turn, reinforce public fear of the homeless and public hostility towards them. For it is the most ragged, the most alcoholic, the most deranged who, being the most visible, come to represent the homeless in the public mind.

What's going on here?

Seeing something is not a simple, direct experience of stimuli posted to us through the letter boxes of our nerve endings. The outline of a man and the sound of his footfalls as he walks down the street towards you are not conveyed in those forms in the messages which herald his approach within your brain. New born infants have to learn to see – literally to "make sense" – of the buzzing, blooming confusion reaching them from the outside world. So do grown-up people who gain their sight after a lifetime of blindness. We do not *perceive* the stimuli which reach us from outside our brains, we *interpret* them. The perceptions are our own; and perception is a capacity we have to learn. What we "see" depends not only upon our nervous system but upon the experience and the culture we bring to that task. Indeed some people have argued that the brain's most important task is, not to transmit, but to suppress most of the stimuli reaching it from the world outside, selecting the few that it allows to reach our consciousness.

We cannot do without the guesswork, based on past experience, which enables us to make this selection and interpret a constantly changing world. By becoming instinctive, this capacity for perception frees our energies to use our senses more carefully and precisely for the few occasions each day which really call for that kind of attention. But we should not forget how much guesswork goes into perceptions. You didn't *know* that the bulge in the man's pocket was a bottle. You didn't actually *see* what he was picking out of the litter bins. You guessed. You cannot be sure. And most of the time you don't have to be: you get by, and press on to deal with more important things.

Since perception is a skill which we have to learn, we can with the help of new experiences and fresh thought relearn it in order to perceive things in new ways. Artists – the great ones – are teachers who enable millions to perceive things in new ways.

Perception is a private experience, but it is shaped by the culture to which we belong. Politics is a public activity which calls for constant communication between people. To talk, we have to use words which represent our perceptions. Words, as we have seen, are not simple messages with a single meaning, posted directly from our mouths into the brains of our listeners. They are loaded with associations, assumptions and implications which will be roughly similar for speaker and listener only if their lives have given them similar experiences.

Words are tiresomely imprecise for anyone who wants to communicate accurately. We cannot in ordinary discourse wring

11

all their escorting resonances out of them; nor would we want to. Their ambiguity and the richness of their texture are what poetry relies on for much of its power.

When we use words to formulate a problem – to decide what kind of a problem it is, and for whom, and how urgent or important it is – we find that they go far to shape the approach – the mental set – we adopt when thinking out what should be done. To call someone's situation "vagrancy" does not immediately prescribe what should be done about him, but it defines certain responses as "policy relevant", and rules out as irrelevant lots of others which might have been considered if we had described his situation as "homelessness".

As a society responds to social problems, it creates agencies, professions and practices which feed back influences of their own, colouring our views about the nature of the problems they are supposed to solve. What may have begun as an experimental initiative by the state or a voluntary organisation becomes an "industry". It has managers, workers, trade unions, customers and associated pressure groups. All of them have interests of various kinds at stake and a set of values which guide their behaviour – a "morality" it might be called. They feel that the problem they have defined is "theirs", and must not slip out of their clutches.

I am not suggesting that professions are only a conspiracy against the laity. If action has to be taken on a big scale it always calls for organisation. And organisations – be they professions, churches, firms or government departments – develop their own interests. They compete for space in the world and fiercely defend their territory.

This rather long story may suggest that perception and self-interest form an interlocking, self-sustaining system which ordinary mortals cannot resist. The world is all institutions and social processes. People come nowhere. The social sciences too often convey that impression. But things need not be like that. By distinguishing its working parts and understanding the links between them we should be better equipped to get a grip on the world and change it. I shall explore those possibilities by showing how people in one city transformed policies and possibilities for the homeless.

Rethinking in Glasgow

Glasgow is not the only city which is making progress with the homeless. But it has gone further than any other city I know; and its story has been more thoroughly researched and documented. In telling it I shall condense into a few pages events which spread over a decade. I shall also tend to concentrate on success, and touch on failure only where lessons can be learnt from it. If that sounds a bit like a public relations job for the city, remember this is not intended to be a scientific assessment. It is a discussion of politics and policy-making; of perception and persuasion.

I shall focus on people often called the "single homeless" – people who may in fact be married, but they are trying to cope on their own without the support of a family or partner. Homelessness of all kinds has for many years been growing in most of the wealthier market economies – even in humane, hygienic Sweden. There are half a dozen changes going on which account for that, but this is not the place to explain them.

These changes mean that despite a growing stock of better housing, both for rent and for sale, there are more and more people on the fringes of the market who get into serious difficulties. Thousands of them become homeless, at least for a while – sharing space with reluctant friends and relatives, sleeping on other people's floors, sheltering in squats and railway stations, or sleeping rough. The great majority get by somehow, keep themselves clean and find a way back into the settled population eventually. You would not spot them if you saw them on the street. The down-at-heel man with a bottle in his pocket, who for most people typifies the problem they may name "vagrancy" or "the single homeless", is only a tiny, if highly visible, fraction of this much larger population.

We are constantly misled by focussing upon the "stock" of people who are today suffering from a problem, and forgetting the much larger "flow" of people who experience it in the course of – say – a year. The stock is recruited from the flow, and consists largely of the (generally rather unusual) people who don't find a way out of the problem. If we look only at them – or, indeed, only at their more visible representatives – we shall not understand what we are dealing with.

In Glasgow people studied those who became homeless over a period of time – the flow. They found, as has everyone who has made such studies in Britain, that most of the people who become homeless in the course of a year are young, and a high proportion are women. The most typical representative of the flow is not a middle-aged man, but a boy or girl in their teens or early twenties. They then took a lot of trouble to find and talk with those currently living on the streets. Most of them were older men sleeping in large hostels; but there were women too. They did not like hostels. The great majority wanted to live in ordinary housing, which in Glasgow usually means a council flat. But the longer they lived in hostels, the less determined they became to leave. By confining people to institutional life, and so preventing them from learning housekeeping skills, hostels create a permanent demand for their own services.

The picture of the homeless which emerged from these studies showed them to be ordinary people. There were between two and three thousand of them. Most had lived for at least ten years in and around the city, and most were born there or not far away. They had as much right to use the city's services as any other citizen. Most were registered with a local GP. The lack of a home was their only common problem – that, and poverty. Most of them were unemployed, but very few had been in prison or in mental hospital, and few were ill or alcoholic. Most had become homeless through the breakdown of relationships with family or friends. Many had no experience of running a home of their own. Millions of other people go through the same experiences, but most can afford to make a home of some kind for themselves. These were the few who, for the time being, were unable to do that.

New policies were built on these findings. Higher priority on the waiting lists for entry to council housing was sought for single people of all kinds. Already the District Housing Department and the Region's Social Work Department had set up special units to help homeless families. Separate units were set up in both authorities to help single homeless people. The hostel residents were given better opportunities for getting into council flats – and not only in the unpopular, hard-to-let neighbourhoods. The city started rehousing them in many different parts of town. They were offered help by a small team in the Social Work Department, and about half of those rehoused accepted it. Most of this help came, not from social workers but from "home advisers" – working class women who taught them how to cook and shop and run a household, and helped them to get social security grants (now virtually extinct) for cookers and furniture. Meanwhile, as the worst hostels began to close, a close watch was kept to make sure that more people were not being left on the street.

More than two thousand men and women have now been rehoused from hostels into mainstream council housing, and the great majority were still there when we, at the University, made a follow-up study of them a few years later.

There will always be some people in a big city who prefer to live in hostels, and they should be entitled to do so – and at a decent standard. The worst of Glasgow's old hostels have now been demolished, and the newer ones are being improved and their regimes reorganised to give their residents greater privacy and independence. As a result, more of those residents now say they prefer to live in a hostel.

Meanwhile smaller special units are being developed in collaboration with housing associations and voluntary groups to make sure there are places where homeless youngsters, homeless women and homeless men can find refuge. These units are backed by the Housing Department which aims to provide flats for their residents when they are ready to move on to them. Bed and breakfast accommodation, no longer used for families with children, has also been largely abandoned as a way of providing shelter for the single homeless. "B&B" is fine for travellers and holiday makers spending a night or two away from home; but as your only resting place it's dreary, degrading, and very expensive for the city you live in. As an alternative, the Housing Department is creating a stock of furnished accommodation.

The appalling old night shelters run by some voluntary organisations are closing, or being up-graded to provide much better accommodation. Volunteers who specialise in helping alcoholics have been invited to work with groups of residents who want their help in the better hostels, rather than set up hostels of their own which are unlikely to provide the best way of freeing people from drink, or of forming good relations with their neighbours. Some specialist "supported accommodation" will always be needed. Meanwhile, pressure is being put on the few commercial hotels which live on the social security payments of the homeless to improve their standards or close. These night shelters and "hotels" are the bottom end of the system on which the single homeless depend for survival.

15

Public attitudes, once very hostile to the homeless, are softening, although problems remain. Much of the hostility was focussed on the hostels – many of them big, institutional buildings – and on the social security office for NFA cases. Both bring concentrations of poverty-stricken men to the neighbourhoods in which they stand. Once it was recognised that most homeless people were equally opposed to hostels, and could manage in ordinary housing, their neighbours found it easier to see them as ordinary people who had had difficulty in finding a home – which is indeed what they are.

These policies have been carried forward over a decade with the help of the Glasgow Council for the Single Homeless, a charity founded and staffed by the Housing Department which also raises its own funds and appoints its own workers to do research and run a housing association. It now also receives funds from Strathclyde Regional Council and the central government and employs over twenty staff – mainly to provide emergency accommodation for homeless young people. This Council includes representatives of the two local authorities – including first rate politicians and officials – as well as representatives of the health and social security services, the voluntary providers of services for the homeless (Salvation Army, Simon Community, Alcoholics Anonymous, and so on) and the voluntary pressure groups (Shelter, the Scottish Council for the Single Homeless, and so on). The University has played a useful part too, particularly in doing research for the Council and helping to raise funds for this work.

The Council for the Single Homeless has no powers to compel its members to do anything, but it has nevertheless gained a good deal of authority. Its members generally bring before it any plans they have for new initiatives in this field. Some proposals emerge radically changed by the critical analysis which they are given at these meetings. The Salvation Army's plan for a new hostel was sent back to its London headquarters for fundamental redesign. Even if the Army's spokesman had not been convinced by the arguments he had heard round the table, his original plan would have been most unlikely to secure the funding it required from the Housing Corporation, because the Corporation would have consulted several of the people at that table before offering a loan. Later, Glasgow District Council, which was contemplating the purchase of a tatty commercial hotel for continued use by the homeless, was persuaded by the Council for the Single Homeless to abandon the idea.

Although the Council is a provider of services, it is also a sort of pressure group for action to prevent homelessness and to help those who do become homeless. The Council consists of the bosses of the organisations working in this field. But there is another, less formal, group organised by the Social Work Department which runs a regular lunch club for their staff. Speakers who talk about some relevant aspect of their work start discussions at each of these meetings, but the personal contacts built up over coffee and rolls may be equally important.

These policies began by consulting the homeless and taking what they said seriously. That was a radical step at the time. Now that thousands of them have been successfully rehoused, without presenting any special problems of rent arrears, damage to property or difficulties with the neighbours, it seems the obvious thing to do.

But it was quite a long time before the homeless themselves were involved in the work of the Council set up to fight for their cause. As a first, tentative step this Council began to hold its annual general meetings, at which it reported on its work to the press and the public, in hostels, surrounded by their residents – breaking up later to continue the discussion informally with them over tea and biscuits. But when it was suggested that representatives of the homeless should serve on the Council, its members – mostly good socialists of working class origin – found all the usual reasons to oppose the idea.

Since there was no pressure for action from the homeless themselves, nothing could be done. But later, as a result of claims for social security payments worked out by the Region's Welfare Rights Service with the help of hostel residents, £1m in back pay was secured for Glasgow's hostel residents, with another million a year in weekly payments thereafter. This convinced residents that it was worth mobilising collectively, and convinced officials that the homeless were capable of playing a full part in the Council's affairs.

Representatives of the Hostels Action Group, as it came to be called, joined the Council. Their most important contribution to its discussions was not specific new proposals but a healthy grasp of realities which kept everyone's feet on the ground.

"I tell all my people: *never* see a social worker or a housing officer by yourself. Take a friend with you. They behave differently when there are witnesses." Such comments helped everyone to bear in mind the real power relationships beneath the benign surface of their organisations' operations.

This work has run into political obstacles from time to time. But civic leaders come and go, and the latest are encouraging their staff to develop more new ideas and projects. A lot remains to be done. The basic shortage of rented housing for single people is making it harder and harder to find shelter for them. All services for homeless people are under pressure, and the plight of youngsters is particularly worrying. But Glasgow has the organisation, the experience and the will to use more resources when they become available.

Other cities

Every city is unique. The kinds of homeless people they have and the kinds of services available to help them differ from place to place. Where hostels have been scarcer than they were in Glasgow, the people living in them may be more damaged and less able to look after themselves than they are in Glasgow. Each city has to work out its own ways forward.

There are still places where the police hassle homeless people, and where voluntary organisations which try to provide shelter and care for the homeless find obstacles placed in their way. Civic leaders seem to hanker after the powers their forebears had in Tudor times to tie "rogues and vagabonds" to the tail of a cart and whip them out of town.

More instructive are cities with a positive attitude but a different policy. Boston, in the USA, is an interesting case because it is much like Glasgow in many ways: a seaport which built up great industries and huge wealth in the nineteenth century, then passed through leaner times, but still retains great pride in the quality of its public services and its progressive civic tradition. Like Glasgow, it has many homeless people.

Here too, studies have been made, committees have been set up and prominent politicians have staked their reputations on the task of helping the homeless. But the homeless themselves have not been consulted or involved. And the problem has been characterised, not as a question of housing and money, but as a question of disease and disorder. Services for mentally ill people who have been thrown out of the city's mental hospitals in large numbers, and services for alcoholics and drug addicts – these play central parts in the city's response to the problem. It has been a much less successful response than Glasgow's.

When faced with a problem, every society tends to reach for the most familiar instruments in its tool box. If you do not have much subsidised housing and do not have a social security system which ensures that homeless people can get some money, but you do have a lot of good social workers and experts on addiction and mental health, then you will tend to follow policies much like Boston's. If all you have is a hammer, every problem looks like a nail.

Conclusion

What a democracy can do depends very heavily on the public's opinions. Those opinions are not just a mental climate – a disembodied set of prejudices. They are rooted in a culture and shaped to a large degree by reality – or what people take to be reality. If you want to change public opinion, you must change the reality that plays a part in creating and sustaining it. In Glasgow, public attitudes towards the homeless changed when those people were no longer homeless. If we go on housing them in large, unattractive hostels we must expect people to resist having them in their streets. It does not help to preach at people, telling them they ought to be ashamed if they reject your views. Shame generates guilt which first depresses people and then angers them. Depression coupled with anger is rarely productive.

But if my first conclusion is that public opinion must be treated with respect – must be understood with some sympathy – my second is that it should not be treated with too much respect. It has changed many times before and will change again. The task of the preacher may be to tell people to be good. But the task of the politician is to help in creating a world in which it is easier to be good.

People's opinions are rooted in their experience, shaped by an interlocking, self-sustaining pattern of institutions, practices and attitudes. This experience and the ideas it generates are dominated by the larger and more powerful groups within the society. The

19

society's realities are their reality, expressed in their words. Thus if the homeless are defined as "winos", "dossers", and so on, that is because this is how the dominant groups perceive them.

There will usually be marginal groups within any society who are excluded from many of the benefits it offers, and labelled as deviant or sub-human. They are in various ways exploited and oppressed. We shall not understand how things are for them – that is to say, we shall not understand *their* reality, which is every bit as real as the dominant groups' reality – unless they can be given a voice and heard with respect. The advice of other people, "expert" about the needs of the oppressed, should be listened to; it will have something to teach us. But it will usually be wrong, at least in part, unless this expert advice is given in the presence of the oppressed, and the oppressed are free to challenge it on equal terms. In Glasgow it was hostel managers and staff and their trade unions who predicted that hostel residents would be unable to cope with living in ordinary housing. They could not imagine that the services they provided might be unnecessary, or even damaging.

The oppressed cannot individually challenge the "reality", the practices and policies, of the dominant groups in their society. The whole culture and its supporting power structure are stacked against them. They have to make that challenge collectively. To do that successfully, they will have to bring something of their own to the dominant culture. Members of the dominant groups can make that easier or harder. But they cannot bring about all the changes which will be needed by acting for the oppressed. Independence cannot be handed out. It must, in some sense, be seized. The attempts to find ways of representing hostel residents in the Glasgow Council for the Single Homeless only succeeded when the homeless began to mobilise and to show what they could do for themselves.

The oppressed will seldom take collective action of that sort unless they have reason to hope for real results. Anger and pain alone will not move them; they have too much to lose if things go wrong.

Civic leaders – meaning not just politicians, but all those with power in a city's affairs – must usually play a central part in bringing about major changes. Their national counterparts must do likewise if the changes are to make a national impact. The state, central and local, usually commands the crucial resources for action, and its officials have a vital part to play in formulating new possibilities, in preparing plans, and in carrying them out once they have been given authority to do so. The key figures carrying forward the development of new policies for the homeless in Glasgow were officials of the District Housing Department and the Region's Social Work Department, but they could get nowhere without political support. When that support was temporarily withdrawn progress was blocked.

No amount of good will can bring about change unless it is backed up by material resources. Those may take a long time to build up. Glasgow's generally humane and progressive policies towards homeless people are made possible by a large stock of public housing – the largest in Britain, sheltering, along with subsidised housing associations, three-fifths of the city's people. The social security payments which supported homeless people and provided – until recently – the basic furniture they required to set up home were another crucial part of the story.

Voluntary and private contributions to the programme of change can also be important, but they cannot take the place of political action. They will be most generous and effective when the state and its leaders give a clear and consistent lead. The Glasgow Council for the Single Homeless mobilised help from many quarters, but the continuing interest and practical commitment of civic leaders and their officials was what attracted and retained that support.

Although much remains to be done before all the homeless can be assured of decent shelter, this issue is a relatively easy one to tackle. The numbers of people involved are not enormously large – in Glasgow about two and a half thousand at any one time, out of a population of three quarters of a million. The costs of the programmes required to help them are not so large as to impose a heavy burden upon the rest of the community. The gains –for everyone – of helping people find a home and lead the kind of life a decent home makes possible are obvious to all but the most bigoted.

But to do justice by three million unemployed, to provide pensions similar to those available in neighbouring European countries – debates about those issues deal with vastly larger and more contentious scales of action. Other questions – like the reform of the laws regulating abortions, or the steps necessary to eliminate discrimination on grounds of race or gender – do not

21

demand large resources but pose painful and contentious choices. We will discuss some of these issues later.

QUESTIONS

You may find it helpful to reflect on the following questions as a way of testing out ideas presented in this chapter and taking them further.

1   You meet an eminent doctor who says she works at an Institute for Tropical Diseases. Are there any other words which might have been used to describe an Institute concerned with the diseases of the poorest countries in the world?

    If you can think of any, would these words suggest that other professions have an equally important part to play in bringing these diseases under control?

2   Visit your local social security office and look at the rooms in which the public wait their turn to speak to officials. If it's in Britain there will often be two: one for people claiming contributory insurance benefits, and one for those claiming means tested benefits paid on grounds of need. What do you see in each room? What does it tell you about the government's and the public's attitudes towards the customers of these services?

3   In Britain the law requires that town planners show they have done their best to inform and consult the public before any important plan is approved. Social workers are not required to do this. Why the difference?

4   I have argued that oppressed groups, excluded from society's mainstream, should not simply accept and fit into the arrangements made for them by the dominant groups – for that is only another form of oppression. They should bring something of their own outlook and practices to contribute to the dominant patterns and thereby change them. Can you think of cases where this has been achieved? Did the dominant groups gain or lose as a result?

5   You have been doing research on unemployment and have received an invitation to speak at a big conference called to discuss policies for the unemployed. You can see no sign that unemployed people will be speaking, or even present. How would you reply?

    If the conference was dealing with policies for the mentally handicapped, would you respond differently?

6   Why bother about the oppressed, the excluded or any of the other

22

things discussed in this chapter? Why should we not get on with our own lives and leave other people to cope as best they can with theirs? I shall begin to give my own answer to this question in the next two chapters. You may want to get started on it.

2 || *Pain, poverty and power*

What are we are talking about?

That's the next question. But first we must be clear what "this" – the central point of our discussion – is. It is pain: not just any kind of pain or anyone's pain, but pain which has five characteristics.

☐ It can be prevented or relieved.

☐ The sufferer cannot readily escape from it.

☐ It is heavily concentrated among particular groups or kinds of people who suffer more than their fair share of it.

☐ They tend to suffer other kinds of pain too.

☐ Their pain tends to be transmitted from one generation to the next, so that similar kinds of suffering recur among parents and their children, and perhaps their grandchildren too.

Many will be quick to point out that these are the marks of an unequal, class-dominated society; which is true. But that is not the central point of my argument. The relief and prevention of unnecessary suffering is the point.

Exactly what kinds of pain are we talking about? It may be physical discomforts due to illness, cold or hunger. Other discomforts may be partly physical, partly aesthetic and mental – like living in noisy, overcrowded housing, or in a polluted, dreary neighbourhood. Or it may be largely psychological, like the sense that you are viewed with hostility and contempt by neighbours and workmates simply because of your poverty – or your colour or your religion. Several of these different kinds of suffering will often be mixed together, so that it is difficult to say where one ends and another begins. Some examples, representing millions of others, will show the kind of people I have in mind.

I think of Cathy Kelly who escaped from a violent marriage and lives with her children on supplementary benefit (now called income support) on a northern council estate – feeding them mainly on eggs and cheese, and keeping a damp flat warm as best she can by fiddling the meter from time to time. Yes, she smokes. When the children's noise really gets on top of her a cup of tea and a cigarette are the only things that stop her from hitting them. "It's the one thing I do for myself". When she parked them with a neighbour so that she could go out to a meeting of the local residents' association someone broke into her flat and stole the television set and all their food – half-used packets of margarine, cornflakes and the like. Her door was smashed, and her walls sprayed with tomato sauce. Everything would have to be repainted. So she pushed a pram for a mile to the social security office to ask for a grant for paint, waited two hours, and then was told to walk to another office. By the time she got there it was closed.

I think of Gordon MacDonald and his family who live on a Glasgow housing estate. Made redundant for the third time, he went south and got a room in Bracknell, near London. Before long he had a job; he'd "got on his bike". But rents were terribly high and he could not find any accommodation to which he could bring his family. The long journeys back to Glasgow to see them at week-ends made saving impossible. After a few months of this his marriage was near breakdown. He gave up the job and settled for living unemployed in Glasgow. His children have only once, during the last twelve months, been out of the housing estate where they live – to see their granny, seriously ill in hospital. They can walk safely only in restricted parts of their neighbourhood because gangs of youngsters attack them if they stray into their territory. Their chances of getting a decent job when they leave school are bleak. There's one health centre on the estate, open for a few hours a day, but no other doctors or nurses for miles. "So what do you do, if your child falls down and cuts herself badly?" I asked. "You pray that kind of thing happens soon after you collect your benefit money – when you can still pay for a taxi to the hospital."

I think of Pat McCarthy, retired after a long, tough working life. Very frail now and getting deaf, he still speaks in the accents of the Irish West. He cannot read but his wife always answered their letters and coped with the various bureaucracies they had to deal with – till she died, nine months ago. Pat lives on alone, in a public housing estate which has become increasingly neglected and unpopular over the years. When someone stole the boiler from the flat overhead, water poured through his ceilings for weeks before the council turned it off. Most of his possessions had to be thrown out, mouldering to bits. When I saw him, the new boiler overhead had been stolen once more. For two weeks he had been living under dripping ceilings; his bed in one dry corner, his television set in another, and one light still working. His doctor, a home help and a health visitor had all written notes to the Housing Department about his plight. But nothing had been done. Eventually his neighbours marched in a body to the Housing office and got some action.

I could run on: about old people who spend large parts of the day in bed during the winter because that's the only way they can keep warm; about girls who've never had a completely new set of clothes; about lads whose job prospects can never offer them the chance of having a car or a motor bike of their own. (Do you wonder that they steal yours? – or go shop-lifting?) And it's all still going on, tonight; as you and I sleep comfortably in our beds.

Pain, poverty and power

People with low incomes live a precarious life, having nothing in reserve. They can cope until some disaster hits them: redundancy, serious illness, the birth of a handicapped child, divorce, a burglary, or a flooded flat. Whether they can surmount the disaster and survive with self-respect then depends on the rest of us – through the benefits, the training, the care and support they get from the state, or through collective action by the neighbours.

A progressive, changing world is bound to be insecure: skills become obsolete, factories close, new jobs for people with new skills open up – but in other parts of the country. It is the least skilled, the young, the old, and the low paid workers with several children – in short, the poor – who suffer most of the insecurity inflicted by change. They have fewer skills in reserve, less capital and credit, less chance of moving out of poverty-stricken neighbourhoods, less capacity to confront negligent or hostile authorities and gain their rights; less political "clout".

If we are concerned about poverty we cannot draw a ring fence around the people in work and say that poverty begins outside it, afflicting only the unemployed, the sick and the pensioners. Neither can we say that poverty is the responsibility only of social security Ministries and other departments of government set up to deal with the poor. Gordon MacDonald's job won't support his family because it is in an area where there are not enough houses at a price which workers like him can afford.

Thus what goes on in the labour market, the housing market, the town planning system and in many other spheres all plays a part in making life tolerable or intolerable for vulnerable people. The benefits which the Kellys and the MacDonalds have to live on are held down partly because there are other men in their streets working hard at rough jobs who may be earning little more than they get. The incomes which low paid workers with several children get from wages and family benefits impose a political ceiling on the payments which governments feel able to make to people not in work. If their benefits go too high, politicians will get into trouble on the doorsteps next time there is a general election.

The British government is deliberately reducing the real value of child benefits, relying instead on means-tested family credits which fail to reach half the people entitled to them. It is deliberately weakening trade unions and cutting back the machinery built up over many years to enforce adequate minimum wages. Thus it is pushing that political ceiling down by reducing the incomes of the working poor. And that affects everyone living on benefits, because the payments made to couples without children and to pensioners living on their own have to be still lower than those paid to families with children.

If you are concerned about pain, defined as it was at the beginning of this chapter, then you must also be concerned about poverty, because the poor suffer more than their fair share of pain. You must be concerned about power, too, because the poor are not excluded from the benefits of an affluent economy by accident; they are the people whom the private sector and the state can most easily neglect without disaster to themselves.

These are the customers for whom it is not worth opening a decent shop, or a branch of a building society or a bank: there's not enough money to be made out of them. When public services are under pressure, these are the people whose mail deliveries, plumbing repairs and refuse collections can be neglected because

27

they are less likely than the rich to complain. (And if they do complain – so what?) If schools or hospitals have to be closed, it is those which serve these neighbourhoods that are most likely to go. If new jobs have to be filled, it is applicants from here who are least likely to get them.

These patterns remind us that pain is linked to one more factor: low public esteem – or stigma.

Pain, poverty, powerlessness and stigma go together, as we shall see again and again. Anyone who wishes to relieve one of these must also tackle the others. To work on any of them in isolation from the others will prove to be self-defeating. Of these four, poverty is the most clearly defined. So what does it mean?

The meaning of poverty

If you ask a representative sample of the British people what they mean by poverty you unearth a cross-section of the strata of memories laid down through our history. Some people define it as starvation and destitution, which was probably the answer that most people would have given in the middle of the nineteenth century.

A large group talk rather vaguely about "subsistence" and being unable to buy "the things you really need". That view first appeared in research studies around the beginning of this century, and a few years later in arguments that the social services should provide an assured minimum standard of living for all. But it was only accepted by the government at the end of the Second World War.

There is a growing proportion of people – but still a minority – who define poverty as being unable to have the things which other people "regard as necessities" or "take for granted". This relative view of poverty is a very old one – Adam Smith defined it in that way – but it did not become common currency in the academic world till the mid-1960s. It made its first appearance in official documents a dozen years later in the annual reports of the Supplementary Benefits Commission, but has been firmly rejected by the present government.

Poverty, in the "relative" sense, means the situation of those who are unwillingly excluded from the opportunities and living standards which the rest of the population regard as necessities.

By tying the meaning of poverty to the evolving living standards of a nation's population, this definition makes it clear that poverty can only be reduced by narrowing the range of incomes within the country concerned. But this does not mean that any evidence of inequality shows there must be poverty about. We must define more carefully where poverty begins and ends. We must demonstrate the link between these income levels and the real hardships which constitute poverty. I shall show how that can be done, with help from recent research – particularly by Joanna Mack and Stuart Lansley who built on Peter Townsend's earlier pioneering work.

We must start by defining "necessities". That task must be tackled democratically, by identifying through a national survey what people in the country concerned regard as "necessities". Mack and Lansley's study of the British described these as the things "which you think are necessary, and which all adults should be able to afford and which they should not have to do without". This captures the essential things we need to know. The list will vary from one kind of person to another, and for everyone over a long enough period of time.

Then we should check for consistency. Is there a broadly-based consensus with variations which seem modest and readily understandable? For example, are parents of young children more likely than the childless to include washing machines in their list? (Yes, in Britain, they are.) If there is no general agreement (as we should find if we put together answers from India, Iceland and Britain, for example) then we do not have a shared culture which can provide a basis for this sort of poverty measure. We should also check that the answers we are getting are not so ambitious that the results would produce an unworkably high standard, far too expensive for the same people to tolerate as taxpayers and contributors to pension schemes. British evidence suggests that our countrymen do in fact agree very closely on a realistic – some would say, Spartan – list of essentials, as Table 2.1 shows. This presents the seventeen things (chosen from a much longer list) which two-thirds of the British regard as "necessities", and compares the replies given by people in different social classes. The next step is to find out who lacks things which the great majority of their fellow citizens regard as necessities. To be on the safe side, we should identify people who lack several of these things. These people are the potentially deprived.

29

2.1 Social class and the perception of necessities

Standard-of-living items in rank order for sample as a whole	AB	C1	C2	D	E
	% classing item as necessity				
Heating	96	99	99	95	95
Indoor toilet	98	95	97	95	95
Damp-free home	96	95	97	98	94
Bath	96	93	95	92	93
Beds for everyone	94	98	94	92	91
Public transport	88	91	91	87	85
Warm waterproof coat	95	88	86	84	84
Three meals a day for children	89	80	83	78	81
Self-contained accommodation	78	76	82	78	80
Two pairs of all-weather shoes	85	77	73	78	80
Sufficient bedrooms for children	74	76	81	69	81
Refrigerator	77	78	76	83	73
Toys for children	81	72	72	64	70
Carpets	59	60	75	77	77
Celebrations on special occasions	67	68	69	72	67
Roast meat once a week	61	61	69	74	68
Washing machine	60	62	72	75	64

Source: Mack & Lansley, *Poor Britain*, Allen & Unwin, 1985.

We should then exclude from this list the people who say they do not want, or cannot use, the necessities which they lack: for example, vegetarians who do not want meat meals, and people who say they do not want an indoor lavatory or other things which most of their neighbours regard as necessities. This will lead to an under-estimate of poverty because some people say they do not want things which they would in fact acquire if they had the chance of doing so. But this procedure (which Mack and Lansley followed) will at least avoid exaggerated estimates. It will also spare us the indignant protests which well fed non-breakfasters directed at Peter Townsend when he included "a cooked breakfast most days of the week" in a "deprivation index" he published seven years earlier.

The people remaining on the list, identified as being unwillingly deprived of things which their society regards as necessities, provide a first estimate of those in poverty and (depending on the number of necessities lacked) an estimate of the depth of their poverty.

Checking for consistency

To validate this way of defining deprivation and to clarify the meaning of poverty we should relate it to other factors. Some of these factors are "inputs" which we would expect to play a part in determining whether people are poor or not. Others are "outputs" – conditions which we would expect to result from poverty or affluence. The more closely both are linked with our measure of deprivation, the more confident we shall be that this is a sound and consistent measure of poverty whose meaning we understand and can explain.

The incomes of households are the first "input" that should be related to deprivation. The household is the proper starting point for this analysis. Its members have roughly the same living standards since they share the same accommodation and organise their house keeping collectively. But later we shall need to look at the distribution of incomes within the household because women, for example, may get less than their fair share, and parents may stint themselves to keep their children properly fed.

The adequacy of a household's income depends on its needs: teenagers probably need more than infants; adults may need more still. Complicated ways of calculating these "equivalence scales" have been devised. The income a household needs also depends on the sums which have to be set aside each week for rent and other unavoidable payments. So some measure of "relative net income" will be required, measuring disposable income in relation to need.

It is here that we tend to be driven back to the technique, most often used, of calculating the poverty line as a percentage of the means-tested social assistance scales, plus rent, for the households concerned. That would be a much safer procedure if there was one such scale, and if the rates for different kinds of people were scientifically calculated. In Britain most researchers believe that the rates for children are too low in comparison with those for adults – partly, because they are held down by the political ceiling we've already noted. Really adequate payments for a family with several children would bring them too close to the incomes of low paid working families.

The next step in the analysis is to ascertain whether the percentage of people unwillingly lacking necessities increases sharply at an identifiable point in the relative income scale. Mack and Lansley confirmed, with their more rigorous methods, Townsend's earlier – but disputed – finding that there was a point around 150 per cent of the relevant supplementary benefit or income support rates at which deprivation increased sharply:

> the mean deprivation score of those below this level is more than five-and-a-half times that for those above this level. Moreover, a given percentage fall in income implies a much steeper rise in deprivation for those below than for those above this level. There is an income level below which people's risk of poverty is greatly increased. (p.194)

If we had a measure of relative net income which was more reliable than the crude figures provided by social security benefits, the bend in the curve which shows the point at which deprivation begins to rise fairly sharply would almost certainly be more clearly pinpointed.

This summary of the methods adopted by Mack and Lansley omits much of the sophistication of their argument. The essential point to grasp is that when deprivation is related to some measure of relative net income, a curve shaped like this:

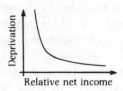

will be more convincing evidence of the validity of both ideas than curves like this:

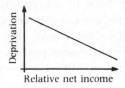 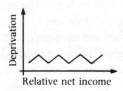

But we are not finished with income yet. Cash incomes of the sort that people reveal to interviewers and tax officials are not their only source of support. So we should check the distributions of other forms of income and of wealth and compare them with the distribution of net relative income we have used up to this point. Contributions to the household's welfare may be secured from wealth, which can be marketable, like houses, or non-marketable, like state pension rights. They may come from transactions in the informal economy, which are in money but not officially recorded – like fixing someone's car for fivers out of the back pocket. Or they can come from the "non-monetised" domestic economy (fixing your own car) and from exchanges between neighbours and kin ("you help me fix my car this week-end, and I'll help you paint your front room next week-end"). Do these transactions reinforce the patterns of net relative income and their link to deprivation, or do they change them?

Evidence assembled by Peter Townsend and by Ray Pahl – quoted at the end of this book – shows that in Britain these sources of welfare are rarely large by comparison with cash income from the formal economy and the state, and that they tend to reinforce, not compensate for, the original distribution of that cash income. Pahl's evidence, secured from a place where "self-provisioning" and the informal economy are particularly widespread, is unequivocal.

That is not surprising. To operate successfully in the informal economy you need information, contacts, tools, materials and self-confidence. It also helps to have a telephone, a car or van, and a shed or workshop – or out-of-hours access to the space and tools of an enterprise operating successfully in the formal economy. The people who do best in this kind of business are usually doing pretty well in the formal economy too. The unemployed rarely have these advantages. Moreover they have to contend not only with tax inspectors but also with social security investigators who are much more ruthless. People caught defrauding the Department of Social Security are much more likely to get sent to prison than those caught defrauding the Inland Revenue.

The domestic economy and informal exchanges between kin and neighbours also tend to develop most productively among people with a few skills and a bit of money. We can't swop help with car repairs for help in painting the front room unless, between us, we have the price of motor spares, paint, and a few tools, brushes and rollers. For someone living on social security to find that kind of money would mean asking the family to go without several meals.

We must turn next to "outputs" – the distribution of things which may be thought of as the result of poverty or affluence, although they also exercise causal influences which mean that they play a part as "inputs" too. For most people their health and that of their loved ones, are more precious than anything else. We should therefore ask whether mortality rates, life expectations, sickness and disabling illness are related to distributions of deprivation and of income – first excluding other influences such as age and sex. Do the poor have significantly poorer health and shorter lives than the rich? If so, do the curves relating these distributions show the kind of kink that we showed on page 32 above, with the poorest people being sharply worse off?

Michaela Benzeval and Ken Judge at The King's Fund Institute developed an elaborate measure of social deprivation which they compared with people's feelings about their own health. In Table 2.2, Category 1 are the least deprived people, Category 4 the most deprived. The most deprived are far more likely than the others to feel that their health is bad.

2.2 Deprivation and health

Subjective Health Status	Deprivation categories				N =
	1	2	3	4	
	%	%	%	%	
Good	86.6	76.7	68.1	51.4	1941
Fair	11.4	18.9	25.9	30.3	579
Poor	1.9	4.5	6.0	18.4	174
N =	411	1076	837	370	2694

Q: "Generally, is your health good for your age, fair or poor? I mean during the past twelve months, not just at the moment."

Source: Michaela Benzeval and Ken Judge, "Back to Black: Deprivation and Health", King's Fund Institute, undated, Discussion Paper.

Some of the latest evidence on health and social class comes from a massive review, *The Nation's Health*, a report from an independent committee sponsored by five of the most widely respected authorities concerned with the public health. These are some of their conclusions.

We estimate that annual excess avoidable deaths in the manual worker classes in men and women aged 16-74 in 1979-83 was 42,000. (p.13)

The expectation of life for a child with parents in social class V is about eight years shorter than for a child whose parents are in social class 1. (p.106)

Findings suggest that 60 to 80 per cent of the variation in death rates is related to socioeconomic circumstances. (p.112)

Social class inequalities in medical care are not a major explanation of mortality differentials. (p.112)

(It is variations in income, environment, lifestyle and so on which account for these differences, not differences in the amount or quality of medical care.)

They go on to say:

> Income is clearly associated with health. The death rates of old people are affected by changes in the real value of state old age pensions, and as occupations move up or down the occupational earnings rankings they show a corresponding and opposite movement in the occupational mortality rate. . . . It is also clear that health is more sensitive to small changes in income at lower than at higher income levels. (p.114)

These differences are not getting smaller.

> Social class differences in death rates have widened almost continuously since 1951. (p.106)

Much of this evidence is summarised in Table 2.3 which comes from *The Nation's Health*.

2.3 Social class and health

Standardised mortality ratios[1] among adult men in Great Britain: 1959–83.

Social class	1959–63[2]	1970–72[2]	1979–80 & 1982–83[3]
I Professional	76	77	66
II Intermediate	81	81	76
III Skilled non-manual & manual	100	104	106
IV Semi-skilled	103 ⎫ 115	114 ⎫ 121	129
V Unskilled	143 ⎭	137 ⎭	
All	100	100	100

[1] S.M.Rs express age-adjusted death rates as a percentage of the average (which = 100) at each date.
[2] England and Wales, aged 15–64 years.
[3] Great Britain, aged 20–64 years.

Source: Alwyn Smith and Bobbie Jacobson (eds.), *The Nation's Health*, King Edward's Hospital Fund for London, 1988; p. 105. Based on OPCS *Decennial Supplements on Occupational Mortalilty*, HMSO, 1971, 1978 and 1986.

It could be argued that some of these differences arise from differences in life style which are a matter of choice rather than a response to poverty (as a poor diet may be) to stress (as smoking may be) or to dangerous environments (as high accident rates may be). If people prefer "a short life and a gay one" they are entitled to make that choice, but we should not blame the result on poverty. If that were the explanation of these differences we would find that the higher death rates among poorer people arise from particular diseases. There would also be other evidence of gaiety elsewhere – in figures for alcohol consumption, perhaps. But in fact the class differences in mortality appear in almost every cause of death. And the rich spend more on alcohol than the poor, not less.

However, we should ask whether the rich are happier than the poor. After all, it is human suffering which is our central concern. If that is not related to poverty we shall have to reconsider our entire argument. Every study which gets close to the poorest people suggests that they are less happy than the rich, although there may be other factors at work besides their poverty. Unemployed people in all social classes are much more likely than the employed to commit suicide. In poverty-stricken urban areas their suicide rates are higher still. There has been a steady increase in suicide rates among men since the mid-1970s which closely parallels the growth in unemployment. But the causal influences involved are not clear: women's rates have not increased over the same period.

Evidence assembled from a vast review of research in many different countries shows that, when comparisons are made between countries, wealth provides declining additions to happiness as it increases. Within countries, however, greater wealth brings a steady increase in happiness – even in poorer, Third World countries like India. Ruut Veenhoven, who made this review, shows that we urgently need longitudinal studies, which trace people through time, to take this kind of research further. By discounting the influence of other factors and tracing people's experience over time, such studies could show whether people grow unhappier when they grow poorer and happier when they grow richer, and help to clarify the causal influences underlying these patterns.

Peace, political democracy, good health, a good education, a happy marriage and personal mental effectiveness – all these help people to become both richer and happier. Thus income and happiness are bound to be related – but for complex reasons.

2.4   Happiness and income. Countries and regions compared

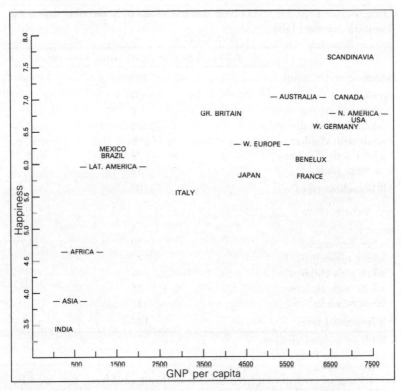

Average happiness and GNP per capita in the different parts of the world in 1975

Source: Ruut Veenhoven, *Conditions of Happiness*, Dordrecht, D. Reidel Publishing, 1984, p.149.

Conclusions

Who are the poor? And who are the rich? Some of the basic answers to those questions for the United Kingdom are summarised in Table 2.5. Using methods devised by the Royal Commission on the Distribution of Income and Wealth which take varying household needs into account, it shows that one-parent families were the poorest of all, followed by pensioners living on their own, and then pensioner couples. The richest were households

37

2.5 The rich and the poor

Composition of the top and bottom quintile group of households ranked by disposable income, 1985.

(Percentages)

	Adjusted to a per equivalent adult basis
Bottom quintile group	
Retired	39
1 adult non-retired	8
2 adults non-retired	8
1 adult with children	8
2 adults with children	24
3 or more adults[1]	12
All household types	100
Top quintile group	
Retired	8
1 adult non-retired	19
2 adults non-retired	45
1 adult with children	—
2 adults with children	15
3 or more adults[1]	13
All household types	100

[1] With or without children

Source: Family Policy Studies Centre.

consisting of two non-retired adults without children, followed by non-retired people living alone.

Within the families consisting of two adults with various numbers of children, the poor have been getting poorer since 1979 and the rich have been getting richer. That increasing inequality is due to growing inequality of earnings, growing unemployment among the poorest, and a redistribution of the tax burden (including insurance cuts in social benefits contributions) which has loaded heavier payments onto poor people while giving lighter burdens to the rich.

There is much more to be said: about distinguishing the effects of long-term and short-term poverty, for example; and about the distribution of income within the family. But my purpose was to show: why we must think of pain, poverty, stigma and powerlessness as different aspects of the same problem; why we must think of poverty not as a living standard fixed for all time, but as unwilling exclusion from the gradually changing things which our fellow citizens regard as necessities; and how such a measure of poverty can be formulated.

All this may sound rather drily scientific. So it is important to remember that we are talking about large numbers of unnecessary deaths; about unhappiness, suicide, squalor, pain and fear.

It is true that to be deprived of what are today's necessities (a bed for each member of the household, and a bath shared with no other household, for example) is much less painful than to be deprived of the kind of necessities that Charles Booth was writing about when he made his first studies of poverty a hundred years ago. But which of those societies – Victorian Britain or the far more affluent Britain of today – could most easily eliminate these hardships?

Each generation converts into necessities some of the luxuries of its predecessors. The heating systems and the refrigerator which most people now describe as necessities are not desired just to "keep up with the Joneses". There are many places where all the houses have central heating of some sort, where there are no longer any shops selling bags of coal, and there is no grocery store nearby. If you cannot go shopping every day and you live in a centrally heated house, you really need a refrigerator – and will, if necessary, go short of food to keep up the hire purchase payments on it. As shops, doctors' surgeries and other services grow larger and are centralised on fewer sites, and as public transport systems deteriorate, there are more and more places where a car is a necessity for anyone who wants to get to work, to the shops, or to see a doctor. As those patterns become more common, the percentage of British people describing a car as a necessity will increase – not because expectations are irrationally inflated but because cars really are becoming a necessity in some places.

These are advances in living standards for the people who can afford to move up to central heating, car-born travel and other features of a more affluent life style. For them, this is what the "rising tide" means. But it doesn't "lift all boats".

We create high-cost environments in this way which cannot be endured without the help of new necessities, and then too often compel poor people to live in them. Meanwhile the rich buy their way into neighbourhoods which are better served by the public and commercial services which make it easier to live economically and conveniently. This is one of the ways in which the powerlessness of the poor impoverishes them. In a study we made recently in Glasgow a colleague of mine compared the costs, both in time and in money, of getting to doctors' surgeries and hospitals from homes in the city's biggest council estate and its most affluent suburb, equi-distant from the centre of town. We found that journeys to these services were quicker and cheaper from the leafy suburb, where most households have at least one car, even for people travelling by bus.

Those who wait for economic growth to relieve pain and poverty have misunderstood the nature of the problem. Growth can make progress in that direction politically easier by providing some of the resources which the poor require, so that they do not all have to be taken from richer people. But deliberate steps have to be taken to bring such a redistribution about.

By asking our fellow citizens to define what they mean by deprivation we bring the constantly evolving living standards and life styles of the average family and the rich into the centre of the picture, and therefore onto the policy agenda. Poverty policies are about the whole nation, not just about the poor. They start from the basic, pre-tax, pre-benefit distribution of incomes. This distribution determines how generous must be the social services required to ensure that the poor are not deprived of necessities, and how heavy must be the taxes which pay for those services. And those are questions about power – as are all the more important questions about poverty.

These questions are not understood by our rulers. In 1979, when the Conservatives came to power, Sir Keith Joseph – one of Mrs. Thatcher's principal gurus and, in the previous Conservative government the Secretary of State responsible for the social security system on which the poorest people depend – published *Equality*, a book in which he defined poverty. It is, he said:

> an absolute standard of living to which the poorest and most incapable shall be entitled. An absolute standard means one defined by reference to the actual needs of the poor and not by reference to the expenditure of those who are not poor. A family is poor if it cannot afford to eat.

QUESTIONS

1   What are the three most important changes which you hope will be brought about in your country before your great-grandchildren are born? Is there anything you can do to set things moving in these directions?

2   Cash transactions in the untaxed, informal economy generally benefit people who are doing pretty well in the legitimate, formal economy, and do not transform the living standards of the poorest people. Try to list all the payments made or received by your household through the informal economy during the last six months, and note whom you made these transactions with. Does your experience tend to confirm the general rule?

3   If rich people are healthier than poor people it may be argued that a more equal distribution of income would not change the average health of the nation because gains among the poor would be offset by losses among the rich. Read my quotations from *The Nation's Health* carefully and see if this is likely to be true.

4   Poor people suffer when they are compelled to live in high cost environments where luxuries of former times have become necessities which they cannot afford. In what kinds of places have you seen this happening? What advice would you give to politicians, town planners, architects, housing managers and others to help them to prevent that?

5   Look at the list of "necessities" in Table 2.1. In twenty years' time, what changes would you expect to see in this list? What kinds of people might suffer because they cannot get the new necessities you expect to appear on the list? Can anything be done to help them?

6   This book sometimes sounds like a sermon. Do the points of view expressed in it have any convincing authority, or are they just the author's prejudices? That's the question I turn to in the next chapter. You may want to get started on it.

3 | By what authority?

By what authority does anyone tell their fellow citizens what kind of society they should be striving to create? There was a time when people looked to God for the answers to such questions. Some still do. But since the eighteenth century European philosophers have laid increasing emphasis on the rights of individuals to make such choices for themselves. Indeed, a society and the rules governing it came to be seen by many as the product of a contract negotiated between citizens – a contract justified only for so long as the benefits which the society confers on them outweigh the disadvantages of abiding by its laws. By the end of the nineteenth century Nietzsche, the German philosopher, was saying that "God is dead".

In the middle of the present century those who dominated philosophy in the English-speaking world regarded moral pronouncements, or "value judgments", as little more than approving or disapproving noises – assertions of personal preference or taste, much like the words we use when choosing between vanilla and strawberry ice-cream. To be sure, these judgments dealt with questions more important and more complicated than strawberry and vanilla; but their logical character was no different. A.J. Ayer, regarded as the leading philosopher of that school, still held this view to the end of his life, concluding in one of his last books that "next to nothing, beyond the conveyance of some emotive and prescriptive force, is to be extracted from the meaning of moral terms, once they are dissociated from established standards". That, I shall argue, is roughly true. But it is the beginning, not the end, of the story. How "standards" get "established" and how they get changed remain interesting questions.

This is sometimes called the "emotivist" standpoint. It was the dominant view in Britain at the time when the people who write

42

the text books now widely used in the social sciences were themselves students. They learnt that there can be no such thing as a value-free science. But they are unsure what to make of that discovery, for they have no way of deciding whose values are best. So they find ways of avoiding the problem.

Most economists, for example, take people's preferences or "tastes" as a starting point for measuring economic values, and therefore as the foundation of their own work. They recognise that tastes may change, and therefore the prices which people are willing to pay for some goods tend to rise, while those they pay for others tend to fall. But they rarely question why and how those changes come about; and they are reluctant even to consider, in their "professional" capacity, whether some tastes are better than others. Other social scientists are usually no braver.

An academic culture

To fill the empty intellectual spaces left by this abandonment of moral responsibilities, an academic folk culture has grown up which – like all cultures – is difficult to pin down, being made up of things taken for granted rather than made explicit. Although their tutors may not frankly teach them these things, students learn that there are three kinds of statement:

☐ *analytical statements*, which deal with self-contained, logical systems, like mathematics: "$2-1=1$" would be an example;

☐ *empirical statements*, which deal with "facts": "two men were attacking another man" would be an example; and

☐ *moral statements*, which deal with "values": "Two against one is unfair" would be an example.

To test the first, analytical, type of statement you ask "Is it logical? Is it consistent with the rules of the system of discourse to which it belongs?" To test the second, empirical, type, you ask "Is it true? Or at least not yet proved untrue?" And of the third, moral, type of statement you ask, more vaguely "Is it acceptable?"

The most respected way of arguing with people in the seminars held in universities is to adopt an analytical strategy and demonstrate that your opponents are being illogical, inconsistent

43

within the terms of their own arguments – contradicting themselves even. Next best is an empirical argument demonstrating that they have got their facts wrong, or missed out important facts which should be taken into account. But that is a rather inconclusive strategy, for it is always possible to dig up more facts and interpret old ones in new ways. Disciplines which specialise in analysis therefore tend to be accorded higher status than those which get bogged down in a lot of facts (pure rather than applied mathematics; economic theory rather than economic history; "hard" science rather than "social" science).

As for moral dispute – that has been banished from the lecture rooms altogether, for it leads people on to say things like "You ought to be ashamed of yourself", and this is not the kind of thing you say in a seminar. To make the distinction unmistakably clear, politicians and priests are brought into such academies from time to time to conduct moral debate; but on a one-off basis, usually at the invitation of student societies, speaking from a different kind of platform – thereby exposing to everybody the unscientific status of their pronouncements. Aesthetic arguments have been treated in much the same way as moral arguments. A whole library of research was assembled on housing, for example, which said practically nothing about what the houses actually looked and smelled like. A disparaging term was even coined to ridicule those who thought these things were important: they were called "environmental determinists". Yet it was often these aspects of the houses – the things which had been written out of the research agenda – which people eventually revolted against.

This culture helps to keep the peace between colleagues and gives academics a secure, if strictly limited, authority. It also prevents the Secretary of State and the popular press from intruding too much into their work. (Look at what happened to schools when their teachers tried to bring moral aspects of sexual behaviour and nuclear warfare into the classroom). But it encourages academics to subdivide their disciplines into increasingly narrow specialisms so that they can operate within their own logical rules, talk their own language, and thereby achieve the highest analytical rigour. Many of them would defend this culture by saying that statements about what *is* never imply any conclusion about what *ought* to be; that facts never prescribe values, and that the purest rationality can only be achieved if scholarship is cleansed of passion. What their students too often learn is that, whereas they should be fussy about their facts and rigorous in analysing them, any value they fancy will do. Their passions need not be disciplined by reason.

Practical implications

The culture developed in our universities spills out into the wider world conferring respect on some disciplines rather than others, and encouraging "practical", "hard headed" men to suppress feeling and avoid moral argument.

Compare the two words "analyse" and "moralise"; or the words we use to describe two kinds of expert: "scientist" and "aesthete". Which confer most respect? More frankly hostile words are coined to disparage the "shrill", "unsound", "bleeding hearts" who insist on posing moral questions. The women who refused to be cowed by this culture and demanded fresh thinking – essentially moral thinking – about Britain's reliance on nuclear weapons were contemptuously dismissed by our Secretary of State for Defence as having "woolly minds in woolly hats".

You can watch the two-way traffic moving across the bridges between the academic and the wider worlds. Compare the knobbly, original works of the great scholars (Keynes, for example) with the text books in which their successors formalise and tame their theories and wring the moral implications out of them, so as to make them a suitable training for children of the middle classes who want to become Treasury officials and stockbrokers. Look at what happened to David Sheppard, the Anglican Bishop of Liverpool, who dared to talk about the plight of the unemployed. He was resoundingly ticked off for trespassing on the economists' cabbage patch – not by economists but in a publication of the Society for the Promotion of Christian Knowledge which told him that "the causes of unemployment are a technical matter where the Church and the Bishop have no special competence." If the Bishop had pronounced on abortion, premarital sex or gay vicars, that would presumably have been "Christian knowledge" – the cabbage patch we reserve for the Church.

This is all part of the culture of the market now commended to us. On weekdays we produce; on Saturdays we consume: both "economic" activities. Then on Sundays we may go to Church or view Bob Geldof on television. Moralists, like the Bishop and Geldof, should confine their activities to Sundays and refrain from asking whether unemployment at home or hunger abroad are produced by weekday workings of the economy and of governments.

Our culture is fundamentally flawed because it is based on a mistaken view both of reality and of moral judgment. "Facts" and the perceptions they represent are not "given" to us; both are interpretations we have to make for ourselves with the help of our experience and the culture to which we belong. The words we then use for talking about them are loaded with assumptions and values which go a long way to define problems and the responses to them that appear to be relevant. The widely held academic view, originally propounded by David Hume, that statements about what is never lead to conclusions about what ought to be, is very misleading. "Is" statements do not oblige us to accept a single, specific "ought" – but they do focus attention on a few potential candidates for action and rule out all the others. They also colour our feelings about the situations they describe – and action is motivated by feeling. To call a man a "wino", a "dosser" or "homeless" conveys three different sets of attitudes, each evoking different responses – different responses, for example, to proposals for giving him a home in your own street, or for inviting him to speak at your conference on deviancy or homelessness.

We must learn to recognise the ways in which our values lead us to interpret our perceptions as "facts" of particular kinds – facts which are then expressed in words ("winos", not "the homeless" – or vice versa) which in turn help to reinforce our values. We do not exercise moral judgments independently of perception and interpretation. Our moral judgments are laced with assumptions about the facts and our perceptions are loaded with moral preoccupations before we even begin to start talking about them.

To make sense of these things, we must reconnect reason, perception and passion. It may have been a useful mental exercise for first-year university students to learn to distinguish between them; but to keep them in separate mental compartments and to banish moral argument from serious discourse is to adopt not a neutral position but a particular point of view about the world. Any discussion which is to lead convincingly to action – even to action designed to keep things as they are – must combine all three kinds of thinking. Learning how to do that sensibly is one of the main purposes of education.

Enter the New Right

For a generation after the defeat of Hitler these questions mattered little to anyone but the professional philosophers. We should not exaggerate the political consensus of those years, but the advances made by reforming governments were generally consolidated rather than reversed by their successors. People drawn from a broad spectrum of society shared reasonably humane and mildly egalitarian hopes for a future in which the state was expected to play a central part. And continuing economic growth gave everyone confidence that these hopes would eventually be realised. Strawberry ice-cream, vanilla ice-cream – did it really matter? Either of them would be nice. And in those days it seemed that in the fullness of time we'd be able to have both.

Now, for many people, it seems unlikely that there will be any ice-cream at all. Sir Keith Joseph, the one-time Secretary of State for the Social Services quoted in the last chapter, wrote that equalising "redistribution is unwise, morally indefensible, misconceived in theory and repellent in practice." Rhodes Boyson, when about to become Minister of Social Security – the man responsible for the benefits on which the poorest people depend for survival – wrote:

> A state which does for its citizens what they can do for themselves is an
> evil state. In such an irresponsible society noone cares, noone saves,
> noone bothers, – why should they when the state spends all its energies
> taking money from the energetic, successful and thrifty to give to the
> idle, the failures and the feckless?

Not since Enoch Powell made his "rivers of blood" speech about immigration a decade earlier had senior politicians so brutally overstepped the boundaries of discourse regarded as acceptable in polite society. Powell had been ostracised, but on this occasion many others began saying the same things; and the Prime Minister gave them her blessing.

What their opponents, the defenders of the "welfare state", lacked was not factual evidence or analytical capacity – the arguments of right wingers more formidable than Rhodes Boyson were repeatedly demolished. International comparisons show there is no reason to believe that generous social services operating in equalising ways lead to moral decay or economic failure. Comparisons over time within many countries show that unemployment, single parenthood and other causes of dependency have all risen – even when the benefits paid to people in these circumstances were falling, not rising, in relation to wages.

Progressive people in all Parties were worried by these developments. But they lacked convincing moral arguments to rally their own ranks and contest the crude, but readily understandable, morality of the "new" Right. They had thought – wrongly – that those battles had been settled long ago. For lack of a cogent, forward-looking philosophy, the political resistance to this assault disintegrated, giving the Right – backed by a popular vote of a not very impressive size – a long tenure of power.

Social contracts

Philosophical responses take two main forms. There are scholars – particularly American ones – who have formulated theories, not about the good society itself, but about the rules which rational people would agree to follow in deciding what the good society should be like. This is a tradition which goes back to Hobbes, Locke and Rousseau, philosophers of the seventeenth and eighteenth centuries. Others – more frequently found in Britain – have formulated guiding principles which rest on a basic aim or "prime value", to which they give priority. That tradition goes back even further – to Aristotle.

The most famous representative of the first group is John Rawls, who asks us to conduct a thought experiment which would exclude all our personal biases and thus enable us rationally to agree on the principles for a just society. Each person must imagine themselves to be ignorant of the role they would play in the society to be formed. Behind this "veil of ignorance" they would not know whether they would be men or women, black or white, clever or stupid, alive today or born three hundred years hence.

Rawls argues that the agreement which people would reach if they started from this "original position" would be cautiously egalitarian. Assuming that everyone would be more afraid of the dangers of ending up in the worst position than hopeful of ending up in the best, he asserts that the people making such a social contract would maximise the welfare of those at the bottom of the pecking order. Therefore, in the just society, all good things – "All social primary goods – liberty and opportunity, income and wealth, and the bases of self respect – are to be distributed equally unless an unequal distribution is to the advantage of the least favoured." Such privileges as the just society would permit must not only help those at the bottom of the ladder; they must also be attached to offices and positions "open to all under conditions of fair equality of opportunity".

Rawls's best known and wittiest critic is Robert Nozick, another Harvard professor, who derides "theories of distributive justice". These theories, he says, by focussing on patterns of distribution, are "so recipient oriented; ignoring givers and transferers and their rights is of a piece with ignoring producers and their entitlements." The results will be economically disastrous as well as unjust, for they destroy incentives to produce. He rejects all "*end-result principles*", and proposes instead a set of rules designed to legitimate people's entitlements to property. His "entitlement theory of justice", he says, "is *historical*; whether a distribution is just depends upon how it came about." He does not offer us any real history. (Telling how Britain's biggest land-owning families originally secured their estates – often by robbery, violence and placing their daughters as strumpets to kings – might throw more revealing light on entitlements.) Instead, he chillingly summarises the human conclusions of his doctrine thus: "*From each as they choose, to each as they are chosen.*" If a temple is erected to the Gods of free enterprise, this text could stand over the door.

There is no conclusive way of resolving this dispute. Having different preferences about society, based on different assumptions about human motives and behaviour, the two professors talk past each other. You could agree with either of them if you started from his assumptions.

Prime values

Other authors offer us a set of principles derived not from a social contract and its decision making rules, but from basic aims for the well-being of citizens and the nation. One of the more recent exponents of this tradition is Ted Honderich whose fundamental "principle is against distress and hence against any inequality which causes it". We are right to call it, simply, the "Principle of Equality." "The Principle of Equality, if anything does, stands as self-recommending in moral thought."

On the opposite political side are many who would choose liberty as the prime value on which to erect the principles for a good society – liberty, however, defined as freedom *from* interference and restriction, rather than freedom *to* realise one's full human capacities. Friedrich von Hayek and Milton Friedman are two of the best known exponents of this negative interpretation of freedom. T.H. Marshall and, more recently, Roy Hattersley have argued for more positive interpretations of freedom designed to ensure that people are given opportunities, which they can really use, for developing their talents to the full. I shall say more about these ideas in the next chapter.

A revealing glimpse of the conservative mind is offered by Robert Nisbet, a contributor to the longest British statement of Right wing views on these issues – *Against Equality*, edited by William Letwin. He says:

As a historian and social scientist I would not wish, myself, to declare any single virtue sovereign over all others, and capable of being intuitively arrived at. But if I were to speculate on what the majority of us would come up with "intuitively" along these lines, I think it would not be justice, however defined. More likely it would be *protection* or *security*, followed closely by *conservation* (in the sense of conservation of norms and ways of life).

Readers will be tempted to take sides in these arguments. Many have such obvious flaws that they invite demolition – especially when presented in the brief quotations I have offered, which cannot fairly summarise the years of work their authors devoted to thinking these things out. But the points I want to make about these debates are of a different kind.

The first is that it is always possible to construct the rules for a good society if you have passionate convictions which give you a clearly ranked set of values, or just one dominant value – and particularly if you are convinced that everyone else has similar values, and would therefore be willing to agree on a social contract producing the kind of society that puts those values first. Such convictions give you the feeling that you have a licence to disregard competing values.

Albert Weale illustrates this point. He hoists the flag of a prime value, saying we should create a "political community" in which people can "approach one another as free and autonomous persons". He also relies on the device of a social contract, formulated behind Rawls's veil of ignorance.

Unlike most other political philosophers, Weale knows how heavily people's capacity for effective, independent "social and political life" depends on their living standards and their self-confidence. He also knows how heavily those things depend on education, income, and therefore on social benefits – for most of those near the bottom of the income distribution depend partly or wholly on social security payments. This leads him to demand, for everyone, a guaranteed "social minimum", well above subsistence level – particularly in income and education. This is "the one overriding imperative in the field of social policy".

But what if people decline to vote for this – as they have in Britain? Weale says these rights must be "entrenched" in the constitution. (That is to say, making the wrong choice on this point is the one freedom citizens cannot have.) If the poor are denied this "social minimum", Weale continues," those who suffer severe deprivations from the operation of majority procedures have the right to engage in civil disobedience". But since the reason for guaranteeing people this minimum was precisely because, without it, they cannot engage effectively in "social and political life", their chances of using civil disobedience successfully are slim. It was a nice try, but the argument doesn't really work. You may agree with Weale; but, if so, that will be because you share his priorities and would support these without reading the book; not because his logic compels you to do so.

If we are looking for an argument which will provide an authoritative definition of the good society – the whole bit: a theory which everyone will have to accept, for all times and all places – then we shall be disappointed. God – or certainly that kind of God – is indeed dead. Among people who share our own prime values we can argue fruitfully about the ways in which principles should be applied in particular societies. But when confronted by people who start from quite different priorities we can only talk past each other. It is like talking to people who lived in another age.

Even at their most aggressive, many of the authors I have quoted seem to be uneasily aware of this. Note how often they capitalise or italicise their key words and phrases (*protection*, *security*, *historical* principles, the *Principle of Equality* – all these emphases were in the originals; none were added by me). They

51

remind me of a colleague, long gone, whose lecture notes occasionally bore in the margin the stage direction: "Argument weak. Talk loud."

Many resist that conclusion because it suggests that some of the most important choices they make – choices for which people have been prepared to suffer and die – are trivial, flighty and no more important than choosing between strawberry and vanilla: the flavour of the month. So what does my conclusion really mean? This is where we come to the nature of moral judgments.

Reconnecting reason and passion

Try another thought experiment. You walk into a room full of people about whom you know nothing whatsoever. It's nearly dark so you can't even see them properly. Then another person walks in, and someone next to you says, "He's good". How would you respond? The statement, as it stands, is no more than an approving noise. If you had to respond to it you could only ask "Good at what?"

But suppose you knew these people to be members of an athletics club preparing to run a marathon. The meaning of the word "good" immediately becomes very clear. Change the social context (make it a bridge tournament, or an orchestra, or a meeting of a local branch of the National Farmers' Union) and the meaning of the word "good" changes. But in each case it remains pretty clear to anyone familiar with the practices of these groups. The performance of the individuals and of the groups to which they belong can be rationally assessed and ranked.

That does not mean there will be unanimity among all observers, or that we have been given a black box into which we can feed data and wait for the right answers to pop out, saving us the trouble of exercising judgment. There will be disagreements about criteria, and about how well particular people match up to them. Is McEnroe a "good" tennis player? Is Enoch Powell a "good" politician? What exactly is a "good" mother? A "good" socialist? A "good" Christian? These questions are increasingly difficult, but they can each be rationally debated because they arise within the context of a social institution and a practice which have widely understood aims and purposes, and in each case we can consult a body of people expert in these matters. To say that

By what authority?

such judgments are "relative" is felt by some people to be demeaning to them – suggesting, perhaps, that anything goes. But the evaluations to be made are "relative" to these institutions and their practices; they each have a frame of reference which makes sense of them. That does not make them trivial or flighty. Indeed, it is their frame of reference which gives authority to these judgments, and rigour to our arguments about them.

But can one evaluate a whole nation and the directions in which it is developing? The priorities which seem right for any particular country at a particular time depend on the progress it has already made, and on the progress achieved by comparable neighbours whose experience shows what could be done. To give high priority to reducing coronary heart disease in Britain, where death rates from this cause are among the highest in the world, makes a lot of sense. Our record for traffic accidents, however, is much better than most. To show that Britain has been steadily slipping down the international league tables which compare the health and life expectations of different countries may broaden our concern from heart disease to health in general. To point out, as we did in the last chapter, that health is more closely related to differences in income and social circumstances than to differences in medical care focusses that concern on a new range of questions.

Evidence of this sort does not prove the case for particular policies. People may question its accuracy, or the ways in which it is used, or the basic belief in the equal worth of all human beings which underlies the whole analysis. If so, these are questions we can usefully discuss. They will at least clarify what we disagree about.

Getting closer to priorities, we must then look at conditions within the society concerned. If you were living in parts of Ulster or Beirut, you would probably adopt Robert Nisbet's prime values of "protection", "security" and "conservation of norms and ways of life". I object to Nisbet's preferences in Britain today because they express the values of a poverty-stricken, lawless and brutal world – the England of the Civil War, in which Thomas Hobbes lived and wrote. They may be justifiable in that world. But that does not make it right to bring them to bear in a country which today has the resources and the civilisation to do better. I also object because this morality drives everyone back into the jungle, compelling them to protect themselves and their families as best they can – and Devil take the stragglers. The experience of other countries where these self-seeking, self-protective prime values are

53

most frankly adopted suggests that as the ring fence of locks, security guards and television monitors protecting the territory of the rich becomes more formidable, the external world inhabited only by the poor becomes more lawless. Parts of the New York subway illustrate that external world only too well. But glimpses of the same contrasts can be seen in the leafy suburbs and impoverished inner cities of Britain and many other countries. The point I wish to make is not that the typically conservative obsession with security is necessarily wrong, but that this is a question which can only be settled by a combination of good evidence, reasoned analysis and moral judgment – all three – applied to a particular place and time. It cannot be settled by a logically elegant general theory, or by running the flag of a prime value up to the masthead and calling upon everyone to salute it.

The authority, for Britain, of Ted Honderich's prime values of preventing "distress" and "any inequality which causes it" arises from the facts that some social groups in this country do suffer far more than their fair share of distress, that this seems to be explained partly by their poverty, and that we have the ability to change all that without creating worse problems. All those assertions are questionable and researchable; and that is their strength, not a weakness.

Albert Weale's arguments must carry a good deal of conviction with anyone who shares his beliefs that in a free society we should be able to "approach one another as free and autonomous persons" and that income inequalities as gross as those found in Britain today make that impossible, and could be greatly reduced. But this is not only a moral judgment. It is also a judgment about the state of his country and the possibilities of changing it. Those who disagree with Honderich and Weale must challenge their moral priorities, or provide evidence to show that they have got their facts wrong, or demonstrate that other, worse, things will happen if this country moves in the equalising directions they propose.

The best evidence available on many of these issues has been recently reviewed and summarised by Stein Ringen, a Norwegian political scientist. He shows that other countries, with traditions and living standards not profoundly different from our own, have achieved greater equality without damage to their freedom, their culture or their economic growth rates. This evidence is part of the case which would have to be contested by opponents of Honderich and Weale.

54

Moving the goal posts

This argument shows that "contractarian" principles, applying theories about the kind of world people would create if they had the opportunity of giving unbiased, collective thought to such possibilities, have a fundamental weakness which is too rarely recognised. They are founded on assumptions about human preferences, and therefore about human personality and the ways in which people are likely to behave. But whereas each of us, as individual voters, customers and producers in the political and economic market places, have to cope as best we can with the world as we find it and the human behaviour it produces, governments and very large enterprises can operate on a scale that changes human behaviour and the wants which motivate it. Indeed, their policies are often designed for this very purpose. We saw, in chapter 1, how Glasgow's policies for the homeless, by offering them decent housing and helping them to make good use of it, have reduced public hostility towards them. If we were using Christian language we might say that these policies make it easier for people to "love their neighbours as themselves" – or, in Albert Weale's language, to "approach one another as free and autonomous persons". The moral goal posts have been moved.

We are all familiar with other examples of this sort. While Glasgow "decriminalised" vagrancy, governments in this and other countries have been quite successful in "criminalising" drunk driving and smoking – using education, propaganda and the law to make people ashamed of behaviour which was previously tolerated. Politicians in various countries who have abolished capital and corporal punishment, though they know full well that majorities of their electorates were in favour of these practices, presumably hope that their decisions will in time create a public opinion which is prepared to support what they did.

These are benign examples of the ways in which creative political leadership can change people's values. There are malign ones too. A Government may reduce the quality of public services which a lot of people use. Then, by generously subsidising competing services in the private sector, it may gradually compel all who can afford it to chose the private option. Since those left in the public sector will then to an increasing extent be the poor and people with special difficulties, they and the service they depend on come to be regarded as lying at the slummy end of society. Meanwhile the service they get may be increasingly provided in demeaning forms. All this hastens the flight from the public sector. In Britain today, there are clear signs that this kind of thing is happening in the housing and social security services – and that some people intend it to happen.

For every morality there is a corresponding sociology: a set of social circumstances which sustains particular attitudes and beliefs, and makes sense of them. Thus, as society changes, so do people's moral feelings – by which I mean the things they applaud and the things which shock them. It is the job of progressive politicians to bring about changes which make it easier for people to be good to each other. Anyone who is convinced that all people have equal human value and should be accorded the same basic rights and respect must work to create a society that makes such convictions realistic. Simply preaching at people, without calling for social action, is a waste of time.

These beliefs teach us to be democrats; but cautious ones. To work fairly, a democracy has to be built on a shared sense of community which provides the basis for a reasonably humane consensus about people's needs, and about the limits within which power can be legitimately wielded. If the more vulnerable are not to be excluded and penalised, those feelings must extend to the whole of the society concerned – not only to our own family, neighbourhood, race or social class. When these conditions do not hold – when, as in Ulster, there is no sense of shared citizenship – democracy too easily deteriorates into a tyranny of the majority which is no more attractive than any other kind of tyranny. Thus democracy is an honourable and useful practice, but it is not an unassailable principle or prime value.

Within a society as large and as complex as a city, let alone an industrial nation, there will always be conflicts between competing groups. We are so inextricably dependent on each other that we have to find ways of constantly renegotiating agreements about how to run our affairs – renewing, if only precariously, some workable sense of common citizenship, making that citizenship a bit more humane, so that it becomes a bit easier to treat all our fellow citizens as worthy of equal respect.

The forces of class, status, gender, race and religion – the weapons of the dominant groups in every society – are not eliminated by social reform. Like the Devil in Christian myths, they are always active, finding new ways of gaining power and oppressing other people. If we cannot bring them under control and move forwards we shall move backwards. No society stands still. As unrelated, atomised individuals we perish. As classes, races, sexes or religions at war with each other, we inflict terrible penalties upon the losers and await their ultimate revenge. That is why we depend so heavily on political Parties and governments – the threadbare coalitions which must for their own survival bring together and represent a wide range of diverse interests, and thus play such important parts in a nation's life.

The continuing journey

We are left with something less ambitious, but perhaps more useful, than a blueprint for the good society. There is no way to found such an edifice on a few contractual principles or prime values. These principles and values derive what authority they have from their relevance to the circumstances and needs of the society which nurtures them. We shall want to give priority to different principles and values in different societies, and in the same society at different stages in its development.

Always we shall need factual evidence about the changing world we are dealing with. Then we must clarify the different features of our argument – the evidence about the real world, the moral values and the analytical principles on which it rests. We can check out one feature of the argument at a time – its assumptions about the real world, its moral values, its logic – and amend any which do not seem to fit. But we cannot usefully question everything at once. In this way, we may find it easier to talk to, rather than past, our opponents; to clarify what it is we disagree about; and perhaps to start rebuilding a citizenship which will embrace everyone in our own country, and eventually extend to the world beyond our borders.

As human society changes, so do human needs and preferences. It should be a deliberate aim of policy to bring about changes of the sort that will make it easier, not harder, to attain the broader objectives we seek. Whether deliberately or accidentally, whether for the better or for the worse, the human race constantly remakes itself and its morality as it goes along. They should perhaps be called human "becomings", not human beings.

In Britain, as in many similar unequal societies, the relief and prevention of pain – and the poverty, powerlessness and stigma associated with it – must be important aims for anyone who feels a sense of shock about widespread, avoidable, human suffering. These priorities are becoming more, not less, important. All over Europe, economic changes are tending to create deeper social divisions. In Britain those tendencies have been sharpened by the government's economic, fiscal and social policies. These trends could be reversed. If they are, and if pains and deprivations come to be more randomly distributed in relation to each other instead of being so often combined, and if they are no longer transmitted from generation to generation within the same families and communities, then the time will come to pursue new and more hopeful objectives.

Conservatives are often bored by the obsession which their opponents seem to have about pain and poverty. They should grasp that most of their critics find these topics even more distasteful than they do. Their critics recognise, however, that it is only when we have brought the cruder social injustices to an end that we shall be able to switch political debate to less dreary issues.

Our forebears who fought for the abolition of religious persecution, imprisonment without trial, slavery, the thumb screw and the rack doubtless found those subjects even more distasteful than poverty, ill-health and the other issues which their achievements have enabled us to turn to. It is upon the foundations which they laid that we try to erect the next storey of a building which will still only have just begun.

Thus there is no universal principle which defines for all time and for all nations the good society – no bottom line under which all the figures can be summed up in a single score. We have to fashion our own priorities in the light of our country's circumstances and our hopes for its future. Our fellow citizens' aspirations are always important; but we can, collectively, change those values by making new aims and moralities possible. That does not entitle us to advocate any future we fancy. Our choices have to be realistic, clearly presented and rigorously argued. Ultimately they will have to convince millions of our fellow citizens if they are to be widely accepted. It is only by general consent that the world can be changed. But that can be achieved – provided we do not expect to start from nothing and conjure utopia out of it, building an entire political philosophy from a few first principles.

The human race makes, and remakes, its world, together with its moral standards, as it goes along. That God-like responsibility is awesome, but liberating. It is a journey we make; not an end-state or final solution that we hope to attain. That journey can only be pursued and given a sense of direction collectively: in comradeship, socialists would say. Churchmen use the language of redemption and Christian fellowship to describe the same quest. Both have too often fallen into the traps of worshipping the leaders, the forms and institutions of their faith, indulging in bloody sectarian strife, and thus forgetting where they were going and why. But somehow the journey is resumed.

QUESTIONS

1   If you were asked to list the most important aims or "prime values" – perhaps two or three of them – which you would use in working out objectives for your country today, what would they be?

Would they conflict with each other sometimes? How would you cope with those conflicts?

2   If poverty, as I defined it in chapter 2, and the things associated with it, were abolished, what new priorities would you want to work for?

3   I have often talked about inequalities of income. Can you list legitimate or justifiable reasons why some people should get paid more than others, and distinguish these from other, less justifiable, differences?

Roughly how large, do you think, would be the maximum justifiable difference in incomes for people who do full-time jobs in the same organisation?

4   Some acts have been "decriminalised" over the past century. Others have been "criminalised". List some of each.

What would you like to see added to both your lists in the course of the next century? Explain your choices.

5   I asserted that public housing in Britain and the people who live in it are being stigmatised, or made unpopular, by government policies. Do you agree? Can you think of any other public services where the same kind of thing is happening? How is it done?

6   Like many others have done, I contrasted the ideas of "freedom from" (sometimes called "negative" freedom) and "freedom to" (sometimes

called "positive" freedom). Write down examples of each kind of freedom.

Can these freedoms be clearly distinguished in practice? This is a question to which we shall turn in the next chapter.

4 Rights, needs and duties

The power of an idea

I have now set out most of the basic ideas and principles required for a discussion of progressive politics. It will be useful, next, to show how they work by bringing them to bear on issues which a lot of people have been talking about in recent years: citizenship and human rights.

The idea of rights is a very powerful one. It is democratic. Everyone understands it from their own experience, and can start working out what their own rights should be. The idea is egalitarian too. People do not claim rights to things which noone ever thought of before; they claim things which the rich and powerful, or the people of more fortunate nations, already have. And they expect everyone to have the same rights unless good reasons can be given for treating them differently. That's what the word means.

Yet the idea of human rights is a fairly modern one. Some of the world's great philosophical systems of thought have managed without it. In this chapter I shall explain what it means and how it is related to other ideas – particularly about needs and duties. That provides an opportunity for applying the thinking set forth in previous chapters.

Talk about rights was once the language of revolutionaries. The declarations of human rights drawn up by the leaders of the American and French revolutions were a weapon, designed to lay the foundations of a new, democratic order – a society whose rulers claimed authority, not from conquest or the divine right of kings but from the consent of free citizens. That consent was to be given in return for an assurance that the protection of the citizens' rights would be their government's first care. Loyalty to the state was conditional, not absolute. The people had shown that they were prepared to overthrow rulers who failed to honour their side of this contract. And the rights they claimed did not have to be justified: they were theirs, they believed, by virtue of their status as human beings.

But two generations later radicals had become disillusioned with the idea of rights. You can see the suspicions growing in the mind of Mazzini, the Italian revolutionary who played a part in uniting his country. Writing in 1844, he said: "All that has been achieved or attempted in the cause of progress and improvement in Europe during the last fifty years has been attempted in the name of the *Rights* of man, and of *Liberty*" (using the italics and capital letters which people are apt to employ in such statements). But by 1858 he was pointing out that the mere assertion of competing individual demands leads to anarchy, and ultimately to the loss of all rights: "If you should understand liberty thus, you would deserve to lose it, and sooner or later you would lose it." Instead, reformers must rely on moral education and "the theory of social *duty*". Liberty must represent "the Collective Aim of the Nation". The love affair of progressives with the concept of rights was over – even if they were not all moving, like Mazzini, in directions which foreshadowed the Fascism his country was later to nurture.

Marx made a more fundamental attack upon the whole idea of rights. Like the laws on which they rest, they are a confidence trick. The ruling classes, he said, besides "having to constitute their power in the form of the State, have to give their will a universal expression as the will of the State". . . "The expression of this will, which is determined by their common interests, is law." As for "the classes which are ruled", their "will plays just as small a part in determining the existence of law and the State."

Legal rights also had practical drawbacks. Generations of working people, most of whom had never read Marx, found the law and the courts a bewildering and expensive jungle, dominated by the middle class, where bad things tended to happen to them. Hence they relied on political and industrial action to advance their interests, and were suspicious of strategies which put them at the mercy of judges. In Britain they had good reason for their suspicion. The Public Schools Commission found that 80 per cent of judges and QCs – the top barristers – had attended "public" (that is, expensive, private) schools. That was an even higher proportion than was found among Church of England bishops, directors of prominent firms or Conservative members of Parliament. The senior lawyers are nearly all men too. There are humane and progressive people among them, to be sure. But, taken as a body, these men are not instinctively the friends of the underdog or critics of the powerful.

As the Left abandoned "rights talk" and the ideological territory it dealt with, the Right moved in to occupy it. (That is a common pattern. Revolutionaries, if they succeed, create institutions which are fiercely defended by conservatives of a later generation.) Conservative spokesmen, however, interpreted rights in their own characteristic ways, stressing in particular:

□ individual, rather than collective, rights;

□ rights conferring negative freedoms from restraints upon liberty, rather than positive freedoms to fulfil human potentialities; and

□ rights calling for legal restraints upon the powers of the state, rather than positive action which might change the odds under which different social groups compete.

These principles have in Britain exerted a good deal of influence. An individual who is prevented by a town planning authority from adding a new wing to his house has rights of appeal to the local planning committee and the Secretary of State for the Environment; but homeless families living in bed-and-breakfast accommodation cannot appeal against the local housing authority which failed to provide them with a decent home. Both may have rights to appeal to the local government Ombudsman, but it is notorious that it is the individuals aggrieved by planning decisions, not the homeless families, who most frequently use these rights. Likewise, individual tenants of public housing have the right to buy their homes, and individual parents have, within limits, the right to choose their children's schools. But groups of unemployed people have no "right" to insist that they be found jobs, and groups of dissatisfied parents have no "right" to insist that an unsatisfactory school should be improved.

I do not dismiss the rights we do have as trivial. There are countries where people are risking their lives to secure them. But are they sufficient? And, if not, how do we enlarge them? Or what other ideas may serve us better?

Some people have sought to justify conservative interpretations of rights by quoting the arguments of an eminent liberal academic, Isaiah Berlin, who contrasted the advocates of "negative" liberties (giving people "freedom from") with those demanding more "positive" liberties (giving "freedom to"). "The former" kinds of people, he said, "want to curb authority as such. The latter want it placed in their own hands." There's enough truth in that jibe to make honest radicals feel that they have to answer it.

In the past, too much of the argument has been left to academic lawyers and philosophers, who have not taken the trouble to find out much about the lives of the people most in need of rights. People on the Left have recently begun to formulate alternative doctrines about rights in an attempt to recapture some of the territory they abandoned to their opponents. They have been most convincing when they remind us how the world really works.

Rights and the state

We should start by establishing what kind of thing we are talking about. Rights are rules or conventions which oblige other people to allow, or help, the right holders to gain or retain something – for example, the opportunity to cast a vote by secret ballot, or to practice their religion, or to draw an income from the state when unable to earn one for themselves. They are an essential part of the machinery for putting into practice the contractual principles and prime values discussed in the last chapter. That is why they are apt to be talked about in words written in italics or beginning with capital letters – devices conveying the solemn tone of voice which people use when claiming to wield a trump card of political debate.

But there are no trump cards – no universally valid statements – in this kind of debate. So we must start by demystifying the idea.

Rights rest on the expectation that other people will recognise that they have duties to the right holders – duties to allow or help them to do or to have things. Those duties must be ultimately enforceable by law. To claim a right is therefore to claim a share in the power of the state; to ask that its laws, policemen and judges will come to your aid by compelling other people to do their duty.

States and the governments which rule them are important, but there's nothing mystical about them, either. Every state originates, and will ultimately be brought to an end, by conquest, *coup d'état* or revolution. Their origin may not be bloody; but each begins as an assertion of power, based on violence or the threat of it.

Regimes which rely only on force for their authority rarely last long. All of them – and particularly the newest and the most revolutionary – therefore take a lot of trouble to develop and inculcate among their subjects a set of beliefs which legitimise their authority. They use rituals for that purpose (coronations, presidential elections, military parades on the anniversary of the revolution). They also conduct a continuing negotiation – publicly and privately, democratically or in other ways – with the more powerful interests in their society in order to renew and maintain the implicit bargains struck between these interests and the state. These are the bargains which maintain the regime, and it is from these that rights emerge and are strengthened or weakened as time goes by.

Governments do not merely respond to the loudest demands in the political market place. As we saw in the last chapter, they can also help to shape these demands through policies which help to modify the climate of opinion, and to confer respect and legitimacy upon some groups and issues rather than upon others. Groups which gain a hearing in these negotiations gain rights; those which fail to gain a hearing fail to gain full citizenship – for that is what rights confer.

The kinds of rights we can claim thus depend on the kind of government we have and the kind of state that it rules. (The "government" are the people who rule; the "regime" is the system of government they use for that purpose; and the "state" is an organised community living under one government, or the institutions of government within that community.) Rights do not depend on virtues or deserts, on kinship or personal influence: everyone within a society is supposed to have the same rights and duties, unless their circumstances can be shown to differ in relevant ways. A society's system of rights and the duties they imply play central parts in determining the meaning of citizenship within that society, and in defining who are full citizens of it, and who are not. Thus, for example, the right to vote was, in most Western countries, first given to women within living memory. In many, they still lack other rights: for instance, to be a priest in the Church of England – the state church.

Rules about rights, even when long established, are never unbreakable: every society is prepared to override them (in wartime, for example) when that seems necessary to defend what are regarded as even more important common interests. (In Northern Ireland, the right to trial by jury has been abolished for certain kinds of offence; and people thought to be playing a part in terrorism were, for a time, imprisoned without trial, and are still precluded from speaking on radio and television.) This is a weakness in the idea which I shall take up later.

Positive and negative rights

Those who want to maintain that there is a clear-cut distinction between negative and positive rights, roughly equivalent to the distinction between negative "freedoms from" and positive "freedoms to", usually want to exclude the positive forms from serious discussion, or to treat them with special caution. The negative forms – the right to freedom from arbitrary arrest or confiscation of property, and the right to practice one's own religion are often quoted as examples – seem to be more precisely definable, capable of more rigorous analysis, better suited for legal enforcement, and less contentious. They are also cheaper: because their main requirement is only that people be left alone, they do not call for heavy public expenditure.

To these people, the more ambitious idea of positive rights – the right to a decent home, for example, to an education which will enable you to take your learning as far as you are capable of going, and to do useful work earning a fair wage, is often redefined by those who stress "freedom from" as the pursuit of "social priorities" or "requirements for human flourishing". They would argue that, important though these things may be, they are not capable of rigorous analysis leading to firm conclusions in the law courts, and therefore should not be described as rights. They are also much more expensive. Housing and education services – to follow the examples used above – make huge demands on public expenditure which can only be met through taxation – which restricts the taxpayers' freedom to spend their own money. Thus positive rights are always contentious.

Some would broaden the attack on this positive concept of rights by saying that we could only give everyone realistic opportunities for these things if we were prepared to impose intolerable restraints on other rights and freedoms. Full employment, some have argued, calls for direction of labour, and for guarantees against bankruptcy which prevent economic development and ultimately impoverish the whole country. For such people, positive rights are wicked as well as unworkable. Yet the market economies with the lowest levels of unemployment – Sweden, Japan, Austria, Australia – do not direct labour, or prevent bankruptcy.

What are we to make of all this? The distinction between positive and negative rights seems at first sight to be a tidy one, and life would be much simpler if we could adopt it. But it won't do. It may be possible, as a matter of logic and grammar, to distinguish between positive and negative ways of talking about rights. But they are different ways of talking about the same thing, not different kinds of right; and we do not in practice have the option of choosing between them. Only people who confine their researches to the library – and to certain shelves within it – could imagine that we do have such a choice. Anyone seeking with honesty and determination to protect people's "negative" rights is soon compelled to press for more positive action. If they mean business, they will be led into a more ambitious concern for human flourishing.

Why "negative" rights won't do

Take the most basic "negative" right of all: the freedom to walk the streets unmolested. There are many places in Britain where black people cannot rely on this right. Home Office statistics and spokesmen for ethnic minorities both report a frightening – many say a growing – number of attacks upon them. That is partly a policing problem, but it cannot be solved by the police alone. To reduce these attacks to the numbers experienced by the rest of the population will call for big changes in British racial attitudes. Black people must be accorded equal respect, along with every other citizen; and that is unlikely to happen unless they have a share of high status jobs and of good homes in good neighbourhoods which matches those of the rest of the population. This may not be enough to secure equal respect for them, but it is an essential starting point for the changes which will be required to achieve that. The Americans have been far more realistic than the British in recognising this, and take more active steps to get black people into universities, into the police force and into senior positions in public services and private enterprises of many kinds.

Even when the British have opportunities to make symbolic gestures which would assert the equal human value of all citizens, the chance is too often missed. When race riots began in London, did the Queen go down to Notting Hill next morning to talk to the shaken residents of those multi-racial streets and say, before the television cameras, "You are *all* my people"? Did she go later to Toxteth, in Liverpool, or St Paul's Bristol, to say such things? Has she used her Christmas broadcasts for that kind of purpose? Can anyone imagine that such steps were not proposed? If she and her advisers declined to do these things, that suggests to excluded minorities that the British establishment is at best uncertain whether every citizen of this country is really entitled to equal respect.

How can we expect Muslims and Hindus to believe that all faiths will here be treated with equal respect when one of the Christian Churches is plainly given a lead role in the life of the nation – the authority to crown the monarch, reserved seats in the House of Lords, and the endorsement of the state?

Another essential step required to create harmony between different ethnic groups is a reduction in the numbers of unemployed and embittered young whites. But my purpose here is not to write a treatise on race relations; it is to show that no-one who cares about what actually happens to black people on the streets could rest content with the minimal, negative, legalistic interpretation of human rights.

Another example may help to explain this point. The assurance that you will be given a fair trial if you are charged with an offence is one of the most basic human rights. This, too, could be interpreted in purely legalistic terms. But the Irish government was recently – and rightly – judged by an international court to be disregarding this right because it does not offer its citizens a proper, publicly funded, legal aid scheme. It has now promised to set one up. Again, if the negative aspect of a right (that all are innocent unless proved guilty in a fair trial) is taken seriously it must lead – and in this case did lead – directly to consideration of the more contentious positive aspects of the same right. (If you think legal aid an uncontentious service, imagine that you have a modest income, just large enough to prevent you from gaining any benefit from the scheme, and are threatened with expensive litigation by someone who is fully aided and therefore has little to lose.)

The problem is even more complex than these examples suggest. They deal with cases in which people can generally be expected to use whatever rights they are given. But what about people who do not seem to be interested in what should be their rights? Consider the following case.

The Plowden Committee, in its report on English primary schools, presented the findings of its national survey of primary school children and their parents. It showed that parents had high aspirations for their youngsters' education. Even among the six per cent of them who depended on the least skilled jobs, their hopes and expectations for the duration of their children's education, the types of school they would go to, and the amount of homework they would be given were high: 25 per cent, for example, hoped their children would continue in full time education till they were eighteen or over. The children themselves may at this stage have shared their parents' hopes.

But what happened? A few years later another official survey was made of youngsters leaving school at the minimum age – dealing with roughly the same age group as the Plowden survey, but at a later stage in their lives. It showed that most of the children of the unskilled left as soon as they could. Their teachers may have been glad to see the back of some of them too. But the point I want to stress is that there was no sign that these youngsters were evicted unwillingly from school. They seem cheerfully to have surrendered their rights.

Yet we know from international comparisons that British children leave school earlier, on average, than the children of other nations at a comparable stage of economic development. We know, too, that British industry is contending with foreign competitors whose workers are better trained than our own, and in many parts of this country there are severe shortages of skilled people. We also know that although attainment at the top end of our schools generally matches that at the top ends of schools in other, comparable countries, pupils at the bottom end do unusually badly here. It follows that Britain must be needlessly wasting a great deal of its young people's talents – damaging them and the rest of us by that failure. And this is happening at a time when the numbers of teenagers are falling dramatically: we can no longer afford – if we ever could – to waste their abilities or the nation's investment in them.

Should this be described as a denial – better, perhaps, as a frustration – of what should have been young people's rights to a decent education? Many would say so. If they are right, the implications are complicated. They call for improvements in job opportunities and earnings for less skilled parents (so that their children feel less compulsion to go out and earn money as soon as possible); larger child benefits or educational allowances to help families with low incomes whose children stay on at school; an education better suited to the needs and interests of these youngsters, providing a more convincing link between school and opportunities for interesting work; better housing conditions (for we know that overcrowding and poor educational attainment go together); and much else besides. In short, we are led into another complex, ambitious, forward-looking, expensive approach to rights. No single policy or public service can solve the problem once it is posed in this way.

This ambitious approach is bound to provoke contention. Because it is expensive it will call for taxation that is likely to be resisted. And if such policies succeed in enabling more children of the least skilled parents to complete their schooling, go on to higher education, and compete successfully for better jobs, then the families which now have a privileged route to these things will pay a price in lost opportunities for their own children – and many of them will resist that.

Rights, like equality, are all of a piece: they cannot be genuinely available to all in one sector of the economy (in schools for children, for example) if they are very unequally distributed in other sectors. The pursuit of rights has to start on our own hearths and will not stop short of the Queen.

Rights and power

If we think about rights in this fashion, we soon have to recognise that to talk about them is to talk about power. Said quickly, "human rights" sound rather like motherhood – something that

everyone must be in favour of. But the people most likely to be
deprived of rights are the powerless: the people whose interests can
most safely be neglected by the powerful. And the rights they are
most likely to want will be things which the powerful already
have, and do not wish to surrender: jobs, at a rate of pay which
was pushed up partly by keeping other people out of them; decent
housing, in neighbourhoods made more attractive by keeping
other people out; an education for their children which gives them
an inside track in the race to success.

To make such things into human rights, the excluded and the
powerless have to assert their own reality – to gain attention for
their own experience of the world and make it credible to others.

The dominant groups in any society formulate the political
drama which informs the thinking of their day and defines its
heros and heroines, its villains, its social problems and its public
morality. This is the "conventional wisdom" of their times. It
imposes on the victims of the problems it identifies – on the
people most likely to suffer from these difficulties – much of the
blame for them. The conventional wisdom teaches that it is the
behaviour of the victims which must be changed if these problems
are to be solved. That view of the world reassures the dominant
groups. It has to be challenged before the victims can extend their
own rights.

For example, every study of the question shows that black
people in Britain are less likely to get into public housing than
white people with similar needs and claims; and blacks who do get
rehoused are less likely than whites to get into the more popular
houses and neighbourhoods. Thus they are denied what should be
their rights. People have explained these patterns by saying that
blacks prefer private housing to public housing; they prefer (the
generally less popular) flats to houses; they prefer living in less
popular inner city neighbourhoods rather than the suburbs; and
they prefer to pay the lower rents charged for less popular housing.
They are also more ignorant of their rights, and less well equipped
than others are to get what they want out of the Housing
Departments. This is the conventional wisdom.

But, as Jeff Henderson and Valerie Karn showed in their very
careful study of Birmingham, all these explanations are untrue.
They are a comforting illusion for the well established and the
powerful, but the reality is a story of discrimination against blacks
– discrimination which operates in complex ways and also

71

penalises one parent families, poor families and other excluded groups.

The powerful find these truths painful, and reject them: Henderson and Karn give us a brief glimpse of the long battle they had with the Department of the Environment and the Birmingham City Council before they could publish their study. Had their findings confirmed the conventional wisdom they would doubtless have appeared two years earlier! Good social research dealing with the outcome of public policy usually embarrasses the policy makers of any political Party to some extent. However, the victims of social injustice rarely find good social researchers knocking on their doors. Thus they have to find their own ways of gaining a hearing for their own, authentic experience.

Challenging the dominant culture

This example – and many others could have been given – also shows why charity cannot replace services provided by the state and by other community-based bodies which give some sort of hearing to the victims. Charity is accountable to the givers rather than the receivers – to the rich, rather than the poor; it relies on the conventional view of the problems it is trying to tackle and is therefore apt to get the solutions wrong.

Charity does not offer rights. Anyone who has studied the history of philanthropy knows how humiliating it has often been, and understands why Labour movements speaking for working people have rejected it. Instead, before the state stepped in, they provided help for the needy through mutual aid – in trade unions, Friendly Societies and the like, organised and controlled by the kind of people whom they assisted. They are still doing the same thing – through credit unions, for example.

A recurring illusion nursed by the well-to-do about the poor is that there is a "pauper" culture: a "submerged tenth" or "residuum" (to use Victorian language); a genetically defective "social problem group" (to use the language of the 1920s and 1930s); "problem families" (as they were called in the 1940s and 1950s); a "culture of poverty" or an intergenerational "cycle of deprivation" (as it was called in the 1960s and 1970s); or an "underclass" (to use the currently fashionable term). All these words suggest that there is a distinctive and defective kind of animal lurking somewhere at the bottom of the social structure: people who bear a major share of the responsibility for their own plight; people who must be persuaded to change if problems associated with pain and poverty are ever to be solved. Social researchers have in every generation tried to find this distinctive group or class of people and to trace how their characteristics are transmitted from generation to generation. And they have always failed.

There are people in every income group and class who are in a mess: a problem to themselves and their neighbours. If they continue for long enough in this state, they are apt to become poor. There are people who are led into behaviour which the rich find odd or tiresome as a response to the stresses of poverty. But there is no distinctive, deviant "underclass" – although a great deal of research funds will yet again be spent during the coming years before people accept that. Then, as "underclass" fades from the language, watch out for the next term that will be invented by the comfortable classes to serve the same purpose.

Claims for the expansion of human rights have to contest the assumptions – the perception of the social situation and the formulation of the political drama – offered by the dominant groups in society, and present an alternative interpretation of what is going on in the world. People cannot just be given rights: they must in some sense take them.

The poor and the powerless cannot even enter such a contest as isolated individuals. They can only do that collectively, supported by others who share and confirm their perceptions of the world. Their challenge to the collective wisdom must be based on a robust sense of collective identity – on something prouder than the rather paranoid hostility towards the outside world which may otherwise be the best they can do. Such convictions may be derived from gender – consciously and confidently being a woman, for example – or they may be based on ethnic origin and culture, on national or religious loyalties, or on social class. Often they are drawn from a combination of these convictions and loyalties.

The black Americans who asserted in the 1960s that "black is beautiful" showed positive conviction of this kind. Women's groups who have supported each other in resisting domestic violence, asserting their right to give birth at home, and demanding that society take the offence of rape more seriously and deal with its victims more humanely have done the same. So have gypsies who have sought for their children special forms of schooling, appropriate for travelling families. London's annual Notting Hill Carnival, staged by Afro-Caribbeans, helps to build the confidence which enables people to assert their own values and make their own contribution to the world.

I shall consider later the circumstances which make it easier or harder for powerless people to assert their own reality, to identify their own heros and heroines, and to claim their own lives rather than live out other people's victimising assumptions about themselves.

Rights, duties and enforcement

The language of rights deals with the obligations of citizens towards each other; there can be no rights without duties. Thus, if there is no society, no community or sense of shared citizenship, there can be no rights. Minimal, legalistic interpretations of rights, designed only to secure "negative" freedoms, are often preferred by the rich and powerful; but they fail to give rights to the more vulnerable – the people most in need of them. Since the whole point of rights is that they should be equally available to everyone, they *must* be interpreted in an ambitious, forward-looking, positive fashion; although this is bound to prove expensive and contentious. Rights, so defined, do not offer us a formula for an instant utopia, but they do point a way forward – a route we can choose to explore, along with our fellow citizens, which may make better human relationships feasible.

The obligations required to give people rights must ultimately be enforced by the state. They evolve slowly through public debate and political action, and they can be lost as easily as gained. Together they define the meaning of citizenship, and show who are full citizens of the society concerned and who are not.

"Rights talk" is most used on the frontiers of citizenship, where people are trying to build new assumptions into public consciousness or to defend old ones which seem to be threatened. The meaning of this talk is derived from the circumstances. Thus if you hear people talking about a child's "right to an education" in parts of Africa they may simply be asserting that all children are entitled to some schooling. But the same words heard in Western Europe probably refer to mentally handicapped children, gypsy children, or other small minorities who may still receive little or no formal education.

The frontiers of citizenship not only stand at different points in different societies; they may move backwards as well as forwards. Talk about the "right to belong to a trade union" and the "right to strike", not much heard in Britain for many years, has re-emerged recently because people feel that these rights are being threatened.

"Institutionalisation" is the word (I wish there were a less pompous one) which describes what is usually going on when people talk about rights. They are trying to build new conventions into established law, custom and practice; or to defend old ones which seem precarious. Such talk offers no trump cards in political debate, but it may pose some useful questions about existing injustices.

Talk of rights poses useful questions too. Who is to define the right under discussion and to organise ways of enforcing it? Will the people who need it most gain a hearing? Can we be sure that these people will really be able to take advantage of it – and if not, what more has to be done to make that possible? What duties does the right imply? What rights of appeal? What social movements and what friends in the power structure stand ready to ensure that these duties are performed, and to help the more vulnerable people to claim and defend their rights?

These are the kinds of questions we must ask about rights. Have the people now telling us that philanthropy should take the place of public social services put any of these questions to their favourite charity? Have those who are busy privatising public services considered what rights the "contract economy" will create for its customers? Have those now telling us that we need a Bill of Rights considered what social movements are ready to ensure that the laws they advocate will extend rights to people of all kinds? We should be wary of all these people unless they can give good answers to these questions.

Beyond the nation state

I have talked mainly about the nation state as a framework for rights. Since they depend on a sense of shared citizenship to make

75

them work, that is a sensible starting point. But systems of rights cannot safely be confined within national boundaries.

Every philosophical theory on this subject includes escape clauses which permit wholesale cancellations of rights if that is deemed to be necessary to protect other rights on a larger or more important scale – and, unless there are powerful countervailing forces, every government uses these clauses to suppress rights when its own power is threatened. In Britain we have recently seen a British Attorney-General suppress what many thought was their "right to know" by censoring without explanation a major public inquiry into allegations that the police in Northern Ireland operated a "shoot to kill" policy. All he had to say was that publication of the findings of the Stalker inquiry "would not be in the public interest".

National systems of rights can be relied upon only if they operate within a framework of international agreements with institutions capable of monitoring what happens, and bringing the pressure of international opinion and foreign governments to bear upon states which do not protect their citizens' rights.

Because the nations of the world have such diverse standards in these matters and little need to listen to each other, international agreements concerned with human rights operate best when based on particular regions in which the nations share some common political traditions, and depend to some extent on each others' goodwill. In Britain during recent years the rights of women and prisoners have been significantly advanced, and corporal punishment in schools has been abolished, thanks to actions taken in European courts. The best hope of extending the rights of British workers now lies in adherence to the principles being developed in the European community. A great deal more needs to be done however, if the rights promised to European workers are to be extended to all European citizens, including those who are unable to work. The German tradition, which is increasingly influential in European affairs, is good at protecting workers' rights, but much less generous to the unemployed and the intermittently employed.

Until recently the British have not been greatly interested in international courts of human rights. They complacently assumed that the lessons of Nuremberg, where those responsible for Nazi atrocities were tried by an international court, were for others to learn. But they are discovering that you cannot be both a

committed advocate of human rights and an unqualified supporter
of national sovereignty.

Where "rights talk" works best

Some people think that the idea of human rights provides one of
the most powerful weapons for political analysis and social
advance. When interpreted in the positive, contentious fashion I
have proposed, it can indeed be a powerful force for change. But it
is not a precision instrument. Nor is it the best way of approaching
every problem.

The problems best fitted for a rights-based approach can be
identified by looking at their political context – that is to say, at
the power relationships in which they are embedded. The
language of rights bears the marks of the expanding early capitalist
world in which it was first minted. "Give us our rights!" The words
make demands, asserted by groups of people exerting their power,
confident that unlimited resources will in the long run be available
to meet their claims.

People can make such demands most effectively when the
boundaries of the group are clearly defined; when the group can be
sure of gaining a hearing because it controls resources which
powerful people urgently need; when it is clear what every member
must do in order to get what they are asking for, and clear too that
all of them will benefit if they get it, and that noone else will.
That is why trade unions, professional bodies and trade
associations, often wield such great power.

But these power relationships also explain why workers who
are capable, through their unions, of bringing whole industries to a
halt, find it so difficult to get anything done about the quality of
the water they drink or the petrol fumes which poison the air they
breathe. In dealing with these issues and many others – demands
for safer roads, better schools, more reliable public transport, more
generous child benefits – it is harder to discover a clearly defined
group whose welfare is at stake. Those demanding change control
nothing that the power holders urgently need. If they succeed in
getting something done, that will bring about small improvements
over a long period – nothing so immediate as ten pounds a week
extra in a pay packet. And everyone will benefit, whether they
turned out to meetings and signed petitions or not; so it is harder

to mobilise people to take action. In these situations demands for rights provide less effective strategies.

"Duties talk"

To contest with rights talk the pollution of field and forest by the increasingly powerful pesticides, preservatives and fertilisers used by farmers and foresters is to bark up the wrong tree – to pose these issues in a mistaken way. To say that everyone has a "right" to an unpolluted environment, for example is only likely to provoke counter claims from land owners about their rights to conduct their business efficiently – and demands for heavy compensation from the rest of us if, for our sakes, they refrain from doing so.

It would be more appropriate in cases like this to talk about conservation of the world's natural resources, stewardship of the land and good neighbourliness – the language of duty. Such a debate may not lead to agreement, but at least it will deal with the relevant questions.

Much rights talk is rhetorical – designed to impress rather than logically to convince. That devalues such arguments. Take "animal rights", for example. Do we really wish to preserve every mosquito, tsetse fly and hookworm? Wouldn't it be more appropriate – more honest – to talk about avoiding cruelty, maintaining ecological balance, preserving valued but endangered species: talk, once again, about duties rather than rights?

The language of rights which is so familiar to us was devised in the world which Western scholars happen to know best – particularly in England, America and France during the eighteenth century. It is a relatively modern invention of the countries which became the leading bourgeois, capitalist, parliamentary democracies – countries, however, which together account for a fairly small minority of the world's people. This is not the only language providing a way into the analysis of political problems.

In supposedly primitive societies of the Third World, people's security and survival have typically been assured by social arrangements based on mutual obligations or duties, often without any concept of rights. In many parts of Africa, if a man becomes destitute or dies, clearly defined relatives are responsible for caring for him or his children. And the children and their successors must repay that debt, if necessary for generations afterwards. These arrangements are best described in the language of duties.

"Needs talk"

"Duties talk" is not the only alternative to rights talk which is open to us. Take another example. To talk about the "rights of the unborn child" is to use words to which it is difficult to give a clear meaning, and to invite counter claims about the "rights" of mothers – claims which rarely advance the argument significantly. We know a lot, however, about the needs of the foetus and the needs of parents. By using the language of needs we are more likely to start a discussion in which people talk to each other rather than past each other.

How can we organise society so that the needs of parents and children (born and unborn) can be more easily reconciled? Needs, like rights and duties, can be difficult to define and to place in an agreed rank order. Nevertheless, if questions of this kind are posed in this way, we shall be dealing with real issues on which some agreement may be reached. It should be clear, for example, that honest opponents of abortion must advocate generous child benefits, decent housing at an affordable price for homeless and badly housed families, and easy access to safe family planning services – or furnish very good reasons to explain why they do not do so. (I, for one, am unsure what those could be.)

Whether we take rights, duties or needs as a way into political discussion is a question that must be decided case by case. Needs will often provide the best starting point – for at least three reasons. First, we know a good deal about the requirements for healthy physical and mental development, and the circumstances which enable people to live life to the full. Second, this basis of shared knowledge means that we stand a chance of reaching some measure of agreement about needs with a wide variety of people – or at least clarifying what it is we disagree about. And third, the strongest case for a right is based on the argument that people, in some sense, need it, and without it they, or society as a whole, will suffer avoidable pain. (There may be other arguments too: that they deserve it, for example; or just that they want it and are convinced that the world would be a much better place if they had it.)

Conclusion

If we can demonstrate, first, that people have *needs*, then *rights* can be seen as a useful set of conventions which follow, enabling society to recognise those needs and to build in the arrangements necessary to ensure that they are met. Those arrangements must include *duties*, without which rights cannot be assured to anyone. These are three different, but closely related, aspects of the same fundamental features of citizenship.

The clearest case for a right will call for convincing statements about all three aspects of the issue, based within a community in which people can be assumed to share common interests. Without that sense of community, needs are less likely to be recognised and duties will be harder to enforce. Such an argument has to deal with a whole society and the quality of human relationships it makes possible, not just with the legal claims of individuals floundering in a limitless sea of anonymous humanity.

You may object that in the first four chapters of this book nothing explicit has been said about the starting points for so much revolutionary discussion, summed up in the slogan: liberty, fraternity and equality. I shall get to them in the next chapter. And that is how they should be approached – as an implication of more fundamental aspirations, not as prime movers of the argument.

QUESTIONS

1   What new rights have been recognised in your lifetime? What needs do they meet, and what duties do they entail?

2   What further rights should come next? Besides changing the law, what will have to be done to make sure that the people most in need of these rights can actually use them?

3   I have said that in most societies there are different grades of citizen, distinguished by the rights they have been accorded. Can you give examples of these distinctions in your own part of the world? What do you think of them?

4   What social and economic circumstances help the underdogs in a society to gain fuller citizenship within it? Can such circumstances be deliberately brought about, or prevented? Or are they, like the weather, something we cannot control?

5 As I write, the British Parliament is debating whether to make rape within marriage a criminal offence – as it already is in Scotland. If the English follow the Scottish example, will the women most in need of this protection gain new rights which they will actually use?

6 Your rich uncle has left several million pounds to a charitable trust for the relief of poverty. The trustees want to make sure that they are not misled by "the conventional wisdom" but use the money in ways which show a real sympathy with the poor and a good understanding of their situation. What would you advise them to do?

5 | Progressive directions

Myths of the Left

Cartoons in the leaflets and little magazines circulated by Left wing groups still occasionally show fat men in top hats and striped trousers clutching money bags. They represent landlords, bankers or monopoly capitalists – once the stock villains of the Left. The cartoons may also show, ranged against them, clean-cut young heros and heroines who are the brave representatives of the workers.

Every movement needs its myths and martyrs. From these are derived dramas whose heroes and heroines are models for our own lives, and whose villains define the enemies we should confront. The human cost of these symbols has been heavy, for myths start from real people. Just as the blood of the Christian martyrs inspired the Church, so people like the Tolpuddle martyrs (six farm workers sentenced in 1834 to be transported for trying to start a trade union) inspired the Labour movement.

We should not deride the little cartoons or the dramas they portray. The political ideals they represent were desperately real in their time and place – for poor farmers, in debt to the bankers, struggling to survive in the American dust bowl during the 1930s; for miners and seamen contending with the wage cuts imposed during the depression by British coal owners and ship owners; for trade unionists who were tortured to death in Fascist jails; and for many others still contending today with hardship and oppression. By contrast, the achievements of postwar social democratic governments which in many parts of Europe rebuilt devastated cities, created "welfare states", and extended human rights, were heroic indeed.

But the world changes, and the myths no longer represent its realities. To understand the scale of these changes, stand in the middle of Easterhouse, one of the four great housing schemes on the fringes of Glasgow – and bear in mind that this city produced some of the myths by which the movement has lived. This was where women staged the rent strikes of 1915, compelling their menfolk working in the shipyards and munitions factories to come out and stand beside them. That compelled governments to mount the big public housing programmes which followed. This was the city to which Winston Churchill, then Home Secretary, sent tanks in 1919 when the government feared that the British revolution was about to start in George Square.

In Easterhouse today, where over 40,000 people live in public housing built on the fringe of town to replace some of the worst slums in Europe, nearly 30 per cent of the men are unemployed. The biggest single employer is the social security office, whose staff do not live on the estate. Here, the monopolies which impinge most directly on people's lives are not capitalist enterprises but the housing department, the social security service and other bureaucracies. The only landlord most people can turn to is the local authority. The trade unions they are most likely to encounter do not seem to be on their side: they represent staff of the welfare state. They close schools and social services in the course of their disputes, and resist extensions of opening hours. Relations between local community groups and the Labour majorities on the District and Regional Councils have frequently been ill-tempered, despite the fact that the Labour Party, which dominates the area politically, is genuinely trying to give priority to the needs of neighbourhoods like this.

Meanwhile there are prosperous towns and suburbs in Britain where jobs are plentiful, where wages have for years been rising faster than the cost of living, and where most people buy their own homes, acquire some shares and go each year to places like Greece and Spain for their holidays. Here too, the rhetoric of the old socialist myth makes as little sense as it does in Easterhouse.

Progressive directions

Economic growth however, is not an end in itself. Indeed, the threats it poses for our space-ship world mean that growth has to be justified, every yard of the way, by the uses each society makes of the opportunities it provides. Conventional economic statistics will not do that for us. They do not distinguish between houses built for the homeless and gold taps added to the lavatories of the rich. If we end up only with more Porsches and champagne, we would do better to turn our backs on the whole rake's progress.

In the present state of the world, the prevention or elimination of pain, physical and mental, is the main justification for economic progress and for collective action by the state and other agencies. Pain is most heavily concentrated among poor people. The poor tend to be powerless. And these three characteristics frequently attract public hostility and contempt. Thus – to use William Beveridge's image – there are four "giants" with which we have to contend: pain, poverty, powerlessness and stigma. Wherever one appears the others are likely to be found.

To understand the needs of the victims and respond effectively to them, we must give them a voice which conveys their authentic experience to the world. To do that effectively and make convincing proposals for action, poverty-stricken, excluded people have to challenge the conventional wisdom of the dominant groups in their society. That is a daunting task which has to be tackled collectively. They must contribute something of their own values and culture to the wider society if they are to make an impact which changes the dominant patterns.

When there are more women managing directors, that should bring about changes in management and in the relationships between work and family life. The world will not be a better place if all we get is honorary men – smoking and swearing as heavily, getting as fat, bullying people as aggressively, having the same cancers and heart attacks, while neglecting their children as badly and relying on ill-paid working class women to mind them. If hitherto excluded people simply become assimilated, accepting the culture of the dominant groups and abandoning their own, that is one more humiliation for them to bear.

Some practical priorities

Poverty-stricken people will find it difficult to mobilise for these purposes unless they are given opportunities to gain real influence over resources and events. They will not give the time, or find the energy, or take the risks of public humiliation to which collective action will expose them unless there are convincing prospects that they will be taken seriously and gain something from the ordeal. Opportunities which are only given by favour of the powerful will not mobilise a whole-hearted response; nor are they likely to survive long. People should be given clearly specified rights wherever possible, protected by further rights of appeal. They will not get those rights unless, in some sense, they mobilise to take them.

The logical order in which to consider the question of rights will normally be to start from proven needs – identified by our attempts to reduce or prevent pain – and only then to consider the rights and duties which will be required in order to meet those needs. How far needs can be met and rights extended will depend on the duties which people can be persuaded to assume. That will depend on the strength and generosity of the bonds of citizenship which link people in the society concerned. Governments can play important parts in extending, or in destroying, that sense of common citizenship.

Rights must be equally and effectively available to all citizens if they are not to become another source of inequality – another means of excluding the powerless from full citizenship. Legal rights which are not associated with any equalising shift in the distribution of incomes and opportunities should be treated with scepticism. For tenants utterly dependant on one landlord, for workers who have no alternative employer to turn to, for patients who cannot change their doctors, legal rights, by themselves, have little meaning.

Liberty, equality, fraternity

Although these principles start from the aim of reducing suffering, they lead on to others which must play essential parts in any programme of action for this purpose. A society which is to make significant reductions in pain among the groups who now suffer most must be a much more equal one than those which most readers of this book inhabit – more equal both in the distribution of power, and in living standards.

A society moving towards greater equality may not at first be a more fraternal one. If many people who previously felt unjustly oppressed at last gain opportunities for asserting themselves, the results may be angrily turbulent. In the longer run, however, a more equal society should make more genuine fellowship possible. That does not necessarily mean that everyone will be chummy. There may be as much contention as before – perhaps more. But it will be more honest, more appropriate; less contaminated by fear, jealousy, snobbery and contempt.

Liberty is all of a piece: it will not be extended unless it is enlarged in all of its main senses: in the sense of civil liberties, in the sense of personal security and confidence in the future, and in the sense of wider opportunities for people to make the most of their capacities. The restriction of any one of these liberties tends also to restrict the others. Those advances, too, will call for greater equality than most countries now enjoy.

The idea that greater equality can only be achieved at the cost of freedom has been much peddled by reactionaries, but without hard evidence to support it. The most equal societies often go to greatest trouble to advance and protect their citizens' rights. People have greatest freedom to develop the infinite variety of their potential talents when there are no dominant elites, no poverty, no snobbery or subservience, and when they admire and respect talents of every kind but are afraid of noone. That is a description of a society which is equal in the only senses that matter.

The convictions I have offered here start from a concern about suffering and the kinds of people who bear more than their share of it, but quickly extend to a broader concern about pain, poverty, powerlessness and stigma. If they are pursued with determination, these priorities must extend citizenship and the human rights on which it is based. They also lead in libertarian and egalitarian directions. In time, they will make greater fraternity possible – though that may take a bit longer. The extension of human rights and the famous trio – liberty, equality and fraternity – are not the starting points of my argument; but they are its unavoidable conclusions.

Back to prime values?

This summary of the basic convictions of humane radicals may sound suspiciously like a list of the "prime values" which we saw, in chapter 3, can be great rallying cries for the faithful but fail to convince sceptics who have different prime values. They differ, however, in three important ways.

First, I am not asserting that one prime value is self-evidently superior to all others: I am offering a group of statements which are logically linked to each other in a mutually supporting fashion.

Second, my statements are not just slogans. Most of them are statements of fact, formulated, so far as possible, in a researchable, testable fashion. You can learn from observation whether people formulate and reformulate values collectively; whether economic and social changes lead to changes in ethical principles; whether pain, poverty, powerlessness and stigma tend to be associated; whether policies intended to reduce one are likely to fail if no attention is paid to the others; and so on.

And finally, I am not suggesting that these convictions are by themselves sufficient to generate a set of political priorities. Or that those priorities will be valid for all times and places. Priorities for action demand a lot more reasoning, and they will apply only in particular circumstances. Change those circumstances – create a more equal, free and fraternal society, for example - and new priorities will be needed. It is a continuing journey that we make; not a utopia that we shall come to rest in.

The opposition

To sharpen the outlines of this argument and show that it has a cutting edge we should pause to identify the standpoints it rejects. They are to be found on the Left as well as the Right.

Many people believed that poverty and the evils which accompany it can be eliminated by raising the incomes and improving the living and working conditions of the poor. The rich and the middle income groups will contribute through a progressive tax system towards the cost of these policies, but, apart from that, they have no part to play. By promoting economic growth and ensuring that the poorest people get their fair share of its benefits, some progressives once believed we can eliminate deprivations of every kind. The Right goes further than this, asserting that by reducing the taxes of the rich they will give them incentives to hasten economic growth and thus confer further benefits on the poor.

This, as we saw in chapter 2, is not true. Every generation

creates new forms of poverty by converting some of the luxuries of its predecessors into necessities of the new era. Poverty and the suffering associated with it arise when people are excluded from the necessities of their generation. Moreover governments manage their economies in crude ways (by adjusting interest rates when inflation threatens, for example) which ensure that the rising tide ebbs away again long before it reaches the most deprived places.

The second, closely related error, made by too many progressives of the previous generation as well as by more conservative people, has been to forget that the fundamental cause of poverty is powerlessness. The poor are not chosen by accident or by their own failings. Poverty is most heavily concentrated among the groups whom the powerful can most readily neglect. If we do not find ways of remedying their powerlessness we shall be unlikely to eliminate their poverty.

The results of this error can be glimpsed in a thousand small but collectively important ways in the public services, in industry and elsewhere. Look at the length of the queues of people awaiting the attention of magistrates and social security clerks, and the reluctance of these people, and of the governments to which they are accountable, to set up the appointments systems which could greatly reduce waiting times. Look at the way in which superintendents and janitors have over the years been withdrawn from public housing estates while the opening hours of the housing departments' increasingly centralised offices have been reduced. Look at the factories and offices up and down the land where management and workers clock in at different times, eat in different canteens, pee in different loos.

Do people imagine that those treated in these ways do not notice? Or do not care? "What would you call a thousand dead housing officers?" I was asked by a tenant on the Easterhouse estate. I confessed myself baffled. "A start."

A third error, too often made by spokesmen of the Left, has been to assume that progressive politics are largely about the distribution, not the production, of benefits. The management of the economy it was assumed, can be left to a small elite of Treasury officials and their Ministers. Some people grasped that full employment would give trade unions power which would have to be used in disciplined ways if they were not to wreak economic havoc. Some grasped, too, that if British industry could not be induced to invest more, and more efficiently, the economy would not grow fast enough to provide wage increases on a scale that would secure the unions' assent to disciplines of this kind. In smaller countries facing a more obviously precarious future, and in countries recovering from more severe wartime devastation, political, industrial and labour leaders had to confront and solve these problems together. In Britain we evaded them – while the postwar boom lasted.

A fourth error we must avoid is reliance upon legal rights, unsupported by economic circumstances which enable people to claim and use those rights with confidence. Anyone who takes that warning seriously will be led on to recognise that high levels of employment and scarcities of labour at the bottom end of the market are an essential basis for any attempt to extend rights to the poorest people. And that has many other practical implications which we shall come to in the second half of this book.

We must treat with caution the proposals of those now promoting charitable services as a replacement for public services. Do these proposals show how the power relations between the service and its customers, the employers and their staff, are to be made humane? If so, they may be worth taking seriously.

We shall not expect exploited or excluded groups to merge without trace in the dominant society, but will assume that if they gain full membership among the rest of the human race they will change things in some way – and this will usually benefit everyone.

We shall not accept economic growth or privatisation – or equality or nationalisation – as self-justifying objectives. To do so would be a kind of idolatry. Will they create a more humane society and a better life, particularly for the groups who now suffer most hardship? Will they make powerful people more accountable to those whom they should be serving? These will be the first questions their advocates should be asked.

Conclusion

What I have proposed are "directions", not a destination. If times improve, if pain is reduced and the world becomes a fairer and a happier place, then we shall turn in new directions. Likewise, if the world becomes a much nastier place, threatened by terror and destruction, older priorities may for a while resume their sway.

What we seek is not an ultimate, utopian condition in which we shall all live happily ever after. It is a sense of knowing where we are heading. The idea is not a new one. All who have written seriously about human rights would recognise it.

You can go back to John Ball, the radical priest who said in 1381, shortly before they killed him:

> Ah, ye good people, the matters goeth not well to pass in England, nor shall not do till everything be common, and there be no villains nor gentlemen, but that we may be all united together. . . .We be all come from one father and one mother, Adam and Eve. . . .

Or you can turn to Jean-Jacques Rousseau who in the eighteenth century said:

> by equality we should understand, not that the degrees of power and riches are to be absolutely identical for everybody, but. . .that no citizen shall ever be wealthy enough to buy another, and none poor enough to be forced to sell himself. . . .

Or you can come forward to the nineteenth century and find Friedrich Engels saying:

> the real content of the proletarian demand for equality is the demand for the *abolition of classes*. Any demand for equality which goes beyond that, of necessity passes into absurdity.

Or, from this century, you can read Richard Tawney's book, *Equality*, in which he says:

> What a community requires, as the word itself suggests, is a common culture, because, without it, it is not a community at all. . . .But a common culture cannot be created merely by desiring it. It rests upon economic foundations. . .it involves, in short, a large measure of economic equality.

None of these men is talking about a final destination; a perfected and completed society. They are talking about the world as they knew it, the directions in which their societies should move, and the hopes which should guide that journey. None starts from equality as a dogma – an aim which overrides all others. All start from more fundamental concerns – about fellowship, self-respect and the quality of relationships between people. Their egalitarianism is a natural reflection of those concerns. As it should be for all of us.

QUESTIONS

1 I have said a good deal about making public services more accountable to their users. The free market can be an effective mechanism for this purpose. In which situations are market mechanisms most effective and most fair? And in which are they least effective or fair? Compare, for example, the teaching of secondary school students, and the provision of their lunches.

2 I have said that the excluded should not be compelled to accept the dominant groups' conventions as the price of their admission to mainstream society. Surgeons at one of our most famous hospitals operate on the faces of children suffering from Down's Syndrome to make them look more like "normal" children. Is this a kindness? Or a deplorable surrender to popular assumptions about normality?

3 Pick any profession you know about and ask yourself: Does it wield power over other people? How are those powers controlled and abuses prevented? Could things be arranged better?

4 Do you approve of the honours system under which knighthoods and medals are awarded each year to citizens judged to have distinguished themselves in some way? Could it survive in a society evolving in the directions proposed in this chapter?

5 If in future more women are to become bishops and managing directors of big firms, what changes would you hope to see in the organisations they lead? How about women prime ministers?

6 I have said that oppressed groups have to challenge the dominant forces in their society collectively How should we respond if their challenge takes the form of death threats to the authors of books which they regard as blasphemous? This is one of the questions I shall turn to in the next chapters.

Part 2
Making our future

Introduction

Political principles cannot be worked out in a purely abstract way in the library. They depend on the world we live in; and that world can be changed. Thus any serious reflection about political theory must lead to equally serious thought about political action.

In the second half of this book I take the ideas outlined in the first half and start applying them to the real world. That has to be a two-way process: a discussion of the practical implications of the principles presented thus far, and a discussion of the action that must be taken to create a world which makes sense of these principles.

If we are to rethink principles from the ground up we should avoid the usual ways of organising a discussion of public policy – with one chapter on industry, a second on taxation, others on social security, housing and so on – because this confines our thinking, before we even begin, within professional and bureaucratic compartments which should themselves be questioned.

I therefore slice the issues up in a different way, starting in chapter 6 with people and the small scale communities in which most of us spend most of our lives. Next, in chapter 7, I stand further back and look at cities and the regions immediately surrounding them: "urban" policy might have been the title for it. Then, in chapter 8, I consider some of the same issues on a national scale. There could also be a chapter on the international scale – and in the next edition of this book perhaps there will be.

This way of organising the discussion has drawbacks. It does not produce a political programme with neat conclusions, summarised at the end of each chapter, for a future Minister responsible for industry, housing, or whatever. Those who want to know what the book says about one of these fields will have to search through it to find all the pages on which it is mentioned.

However, it may compel us to think about some questions which more conventional approaches fail to pose because they do not fit comfortably into these bureaucratic boxes. It also helps to drive the argument forward by showing, at each scale, the problems which cannot be effectively tackled unless we also operate at larger scales.

I have gone back to a more conventional approach in chapter 9 which picks one field of policy and uses it as a way of linking some of the issues divided up under different scales and levels of government in the previous chapters. For this purpose I took housing policy because it most clearly shows the need to work at all these scales of action, and to accept that the private, the voluntary and the state sectors of the economy each have a part to play. It is in that way typical of the world we now live in.

I draw the book to a close with a chapter summarising its main conclusions, and a final postscript which asks whether anyone will listen to the ideas I have offered – a question I try to answer by reflecting on the ways in which societies and their politics change, and on the contribution we can each make to those mysterious processes.

6 | People first

Where we've come from

It is the nation state to which the main arguments of the first part of this book have been addressed. Thus it is at the national scale that much of the action they call for must be taken. But those who want to rebuild a progressive movement would do well to remember that there are people, undeterred by the bleak years we have been passing through, who have set about changing whatever small piece of the world they happen to live in. That is why the second part of this book starts at ground level. In doing that, however, we must remember that a lot of important things must also be said about larger scales of action. I shall come to them later.

We have seen in previous chapters that, if their needs are not to be misinterpreted and neglected, the people most likely to be excluded from the mainstream of society by poverty and public indifference must be given a voice and enabled to challenge the conventional wisdom. We have seen, too, that this has to be done collectively. By themselves, individuals are powerless. But how is that challenge to be mounted?

Most of the services of the state are organised to prevent those things from happening. For the well paid and fully employed – the people in the mainstream – that does not matter too much: public services usually meet their needs pretty well, and, if they don't, these people can often get what they want in other ways. They can buy a house for themselves instead of renting one from the local Council, they can pay their dentist for work which he will not do under the Health Service, or they can move to another neighbourhood where the schools are better. But less fortunate people often feel as if they were imprisoned in the rules and conventions of services organised to meet the needs of their staff, the taxpayers, the legislators – anyone, rather than their customers.

Examples of these patterns are to be found in nearly every service. Suppose you are looking for a place, close to your own home and work, where your grandmother can be cared for. Let's imagine she's a ninety-year-old lady, kept precariously alive by drugs, wandering a bit in her mind, and about to be discharged from the hospital which patched her up after yet another bad fall. You will find that elderly men and women like this are to be found in "sheltered housing" (houses with a warden, and a varying complement of visiting nurses and other helpers) which is provided or supervised by district housing authorities. They are also found in "residential homes", provided or supervised by the county Social Services or (in Scotland) the regional Social Work Departments. And they are found in "nursing homes", supervised by the central government's Area Health Authorities. But there is no one place where you can find out about all three, and no single authority responsible for planning their development or allocating people to them.

The three main professions (housing, social work, and nursing) which run these services operate under different laws which provide quite different payments to support the people they care for; and they have different salary scales, employers, trade unions, traditions and values – and will not surrender an inch of their territory to their rivals. "Housers" give priority to people with housing needs, but are less concerned about their need for daily care; social workers care about privacy and like people to have rooms to themselves and keys to their doors; nurses like people to be in large wards where they can keep an eye on them, and are better than the others at storing drugs and keeping things clean. Woe betide anyone who tries to build some houses with a resident warden, and a nursing home nearby, together with a small pub used by local people where visiting relatives could stay, and a visiting service to help people manage in their own homes for as long as they want to and get them all registered and approved as one caring service – which would in fact be the most sensible thing to do! (This and more has been marvellously done by the London Lighthouse – but only for people with HIV and AIDS.)

It is no wonder that when Britain's Conservative government set about privatising services like this – handing them over to the market – it was generally the staff, not the customers, who turned out to protest. The staff were sometimes right to do that: but they will need to have their customers standing shoulder to shoulder with them before governments will pay much attention to what they are saying.

Every public service – and not least the universities, in which I have worked for most of my life – could provide similar examples of the ways in which they have developed to meet the needs of their administrators and staff, and to keep under strict control any demand from the public which might disturb these patterns. Representatives of the public are indeed elected or appointed to play their part in running all these services, but on terms which make them the most resolute defenders of the fiefdoms which give them their function and status. And if, after long years of devoted attendance at committee meetings, they are awarded an MBE, a CBE or some other honour, it will probably be "for services to Education", or "Nursing" or whatever – not for being a good citizen. The twice-yearly ration of honours is distributed through the departments of government which run the system.

There are good reasons as well as bad ones for these patterns. Most of these organisations took shape in times of crisis when governments were extending to everyone services which more fortunate people already had. That was during the world wars and in subsequent periods of postwar reconstruction, population explosion and the rapid growth of cities. The directors of these services then had to work day and night to evacuate children from the cities, to feed and shelter the bombed-out, and – later – to put roofs over people's heads, to make hospital services available all over the country and bring the waiting lists down, and to make sure that by September each year there would be a desk and a chair in a classroom for every child of school age, with someone who looked like a teacher standing in front of them. Every service invented numbers games to measure its progress towards these objectives: houses built and families rehoused, hospital bed occupancy and throughput, average class size and percentage of trained teachers. . . . And sometimes they failed: families were left homeless, or two schools had to work double shifts from the same buildings with untrained staff, and the press made a scandal of it.

These were years of heroic achievement. But they left their mark. People learnt that the way to run a public service was to create a powerful, centralised organisation employing trained, specialist staff to deliver a standard product to all those entitled to receive it. Familiar wartime styles of command were continued into peace time. Later, the pressure groups unwittingly reinforced these patterns. They demanded more of the same resources. And they fought to extend people's rights by hunting out "anomalies" – that is to say, people with similar needs being treated better in some places than in others. These were always described as "indefensible". To defend the system, governments then felt compelled to make more and more rules standardising and centralising everything.

The British are perhaps more inclined than most people to accept these "top-down" patterns of administration. We have not been occupied by a conquering power since 1066, and we have no living memory of brutal tyranny. Thus our instinct is to trust the state and rely on it. But in many other countries people still remember times when local leaders could only survive if their neighbours were prepared to risk their lives to protect them from the state and its secret police. Indeed, in many countries that's still the way things are. There, a community-based, "bottom-up" pattern of public service seems more natural. That may explain why community action tends to be livelier in Ulster than in other parts of the United Kingdom – and liveliest of all among Catholic working class people there who never trusted the Protestant Unionist state.

People in Britain recognised that the old, bureaucratic system had its defects. But for a long time its defenders and its critics both assumed that in time, with more money and better "co-ordination" (a much-used word) these defects would be put right. So they joined forces to press the government for more resources.

I recall one of the moments at which it dawned on me that things were not so simple. More than twenty years ago, as a member of the team then designing what we were determined was going to be the best new town yet – Milton Keynes – I went to meet the heads of the social services which would operate there in the hope that we could set up one-stop centres all over the town from which people would be able to get every public service they needed. The chief medical officer explained that to assemble an effective team of doctors, nurses, midwives and specialist services he must have health centres with twelve general practitioners, each serving a population of 30,000. The man in charge of the social workers gave a complicated set of reasons to prove that they could only operate in teams serving 8,000 people. As I tried to figure out how to fit multiples of 8 into 30, the chief probation officer said he only needed one office and it had to be at the courthouse. Then the penny dropped. Whatever we did, these barons of the public services would invent numbers which would preserve the separate offices and administrative areas which protected their fiefdoms.

Later, as one country after another was hit by the economic crisis which led their rising public expenditure to outrun their flagging tax revenues, the "positive sum" political game in which everyone could win something turned into a zero sum game or worse – a contest for resources in which every winner's gains had to be paid for by someone else's losses. Taxpayers' revolts followed in many countries – most explicitly in Denmark, Ireland and the USA – and it soon became clear that the old patterns of public service were never going to solve all the problems: the voters would not provide enough money to make that possible.

New things then began to happen in many countries. But every system has its defenders, and people do not part with authority willingly. The new patterns only emerged when the old ones proved unworkable and were discredited. But before coming to that we should pause to clarify what we are talking about.

Definitions

In what I shall describe as "community-based" projects the users of a service have some control over the resources required to provide the service. Their control may be complete, or it may be no more than a powerful influence; the project may be governmental or voluntary in form; and it may be funded from public, commercial or charitable sources, or from some mixture of these. The projects I have in mind include credit unions; food co-operatives for joint purchase of groceries; neighbourhood watch associations set up in conjunction with the police; associations offering mutual support to people who suffer from the same disease or handicap; housing management co-operatives and housing associations, if they are run by the tenants of the houses concerned; adult education and arts groups in which the participants choose the work they do and decide for themselves how to do it; and more broadly-based community associations which organise a wider range of activities which may include business enterprises, a newspaper, social clubs and youth projects, a creche, welfare rights and pressure group work, sports and drama groups, and so on.

"Users' control" is not a precise definition, but it helps to exclude some things which look the same, but aren't. It excludes decentralisation of public services which only disperses work from central offices to numerous small neighbourhood offices. It would be better to call this "deconcentration". It excludes procedures for consulting the public which do not give away any real power over the services concerned. It also excludes trade unions which began as small, community-based groups, but have mostly become nationwide organisations with bureaucracies of their own. Less justifiably perhaps, even the more democratic, locally-based churches have been excluded: although they may give practical help to their members, that is usually not their main task.

Those frontiers are fairly clearly marked, but there is no clear boundary distinguishing the community-based projects I shall be discussing from community businesses and producer co-operatives, owned by those who work in them, which trade with a wider public. I include these enterprises if they are accountable to a community closely associated with them, and are primarily designed to benefit that community by selling them goods and services or by earning surpluses which are spent on projects chosen by the community. But I would not include enterprises which operate much like any other profit making business, even if they have a co-operative constitution.

Among these organisations it is those which are accountable to poor people or which operate in deprived neighbourhoods that most interest us. That is not to dismiss as irrelevant the mass of local conservation groups, wine societies, drama clubs, tennis clubs, music societies and the like which operate in more comfortable neighbourhoods. They enhance the quality of life there, but they are less likely to bring about changes in the larger society.

Why are these things happening?

Why are the kinds of enterprise that I have described being formed in so many countries? The distribution of power shifts only when it has to. How strong the compulsions for change must be is made clear by the fact that it is often in the most centralised, authoritarian services that community-based methods were first introduced – the services which were, in the old-fashioned sense, most "professional" (meaning that their professionals had conceded least power to their clients).

In Britain, the army was one of the first organisations to recognise the need for new tactics. In subversion, guerilla warfare and the "low intensity operations" which, in a nuclear age, have become the main form of military action, the winning of hearts and minds is more important than the winning of battles. That calls for new kinds of training, and a new set of military virtues. Stormtroops like the "Paras", trained for the battlefield, made disastrous mistakes when let loose in the streets of Derry.

The police, investigated by Lord Scarman after disturbances which drove them off the Brixton streets, have adopted his proposals for local liaison groups and other methods of gaining support from the public. Crime prevention, which used to be all about burglar alarms and similar hardware, is now all about "community policing". (The police have acquired more formidable hardware too, but that's to control riots, rather than prevent crime.)

Medical services have increasingly come to accept the view, eloquently expressed by the World Health Organisation, that their most important task is not to cure disease but to help citizens take more effective care of their own health. That is how heart disease and many kinds of cancer – the main killers in the more affluent countries – have been reduced. AIDS will reinforce this trend: medical authorities, unable to offer any remedies for this disaster, can only appeal to the most vulnerable groups to get together and collectively adopt safer living patterns.

Manpower and training services, unable to find jobs for large numbers of unemployed people, and unable in the worst-hit areas to induce commercial employers to provide temporary work or training opportunities on anything like the scale required, have turned to community projects of various kinds to fill the gap. Meanwhile the local housing authorities in some of Britain's oldest cities, having completed the biggest slum clearance and rehousing programmes the world has ever seen, find that people refuse to live in some of the houses built for them only a few years ago. As vacancies increase, so do vandalism, break-ins, lost rents and the

turnover of tenants. This has compelled them to turn to the
tenants and seek their help – setting up housing management co-
operatives, community-based housing associations and community
ownership schemes of various kinds.

There were political motives, too, for these developments. As
the Labour Party lost seats in its classic strongholds – in places like
Merseyside, Islington, Bermondsey and other inner city areas –
they and the centre Parties competed for public support by trying
to give the "welfare state" a more human face.

In short, changes are coming about because they have to: the
old bureaucratic systems won't work any more. There have been
similar developments in many other countries. The community-
based approach was only one of the responses which followed.
"Privatisation" was another. Community-based policing was
paralleled by growing reliance on firms selling security services;
community-based forms of health care were accompanied by a
revival of private medicine; and housing co-operatives by the drive
to sell public housing to its tenants. The ideologies look like polar
opposites, but they have a good deal in common. Glasgow's
community ownership scheme which transferred council houses en
bloc to their tenants was "sold" simultaneously to a Labour council
as a return to socialist principles, and to Conservative ministers as
a form of privatisation. Indeed, there is now a real danger that the
old romanticism about the state will be succeeded by new love
affairs with communities and markets. We must keep cool heads.

Community-based approaches

Most community-based projects are specialised or functional
agencies performing a fairly clearly defined task, usually for a
clearly defined population. The housing management co-operatives
set up in Glasgow are an example of this type. They are given a
budget by the Council which is sufficient to employ someone to
serve a committee which is elected by all the tenants of the block
of property involved. With its manager's help, the co-op repairs
and maintains the houses and carries out minor capital works.
Within broad priorities agreed with the Housing Department, it
also chooses tenants for empty houses.

Credit unions, if they are managed not by employers for their
workers but by their own members, are another example of this

type. They are, however, a response to failures of free enterprise, not failures of the state. Some local authorities have appointed development officers to promote the formation of credit unions, particularly in deprived communities where banks, building societies and other conventional financial institutions do not set up branches.

Community businesses, managed by a committee elected by the people they serve, sometimes illustrate the same pattern. One of the most striking examples in the UK is the Galliagh Co-op, which built and successfully manages a supermarket in the largest housing estate in Derry where private enterprise was reluctant to operate. People living on this poverty-stricken estate put together in one-pound shares the capital to get the co-op started. Some years later, after making grants to local voluntary groups, the co-op's accumulated surplus amounted to about £100,000 which was available for developing new projects.

The local branches of lay, self-help groups, providing mutual support and care for members suffering from a particular disease, handicap or problem, are a growing category. They work with cancers of various kinds, heart disease, eczema, asthma, drug addictions, alcoholism, mental handicap, multiple sclerosis, and many other problems. A research worker has calculated that there are 1,500 national organisations of this sort with over 25,000 regional branches – more than 200 of them for eczema alone. Their members may be the sufferers (people with AIDS, for example) or the people responsible for caring for them (parents of mentally handicapped children, for example). Their national headquarters may dominate the organisation, or may only be a back-up for local initiatives. Some only campaign for research funds and medical equipment. Others provide a much more extensive support service for their members while also doing a nationwide job of public education and pressure politics.

All these organisations seem to have been launched by people who were fed up with the service they were getting from conventional medical sources. They then rely pretty heavily, however, on help from friendly doctors and health administrators. These are patterns we shall meet again and again in this kind of project.

Some self-help groups have grown on a scale which suggests the possibility of developing, a broader community association capable of tackling any task the members want to turn their hand

105

to. An Irish group working with, and for, the travelling people who live in caravans illustrate a pattern of this sort. Along with legal advice and pressure group work, they have developed educational programmes for adults dealing with the travellers' history and traditions as well as more basic skills of literacy, and have involved the travellers themselves in planning and developing the project. Distinctive ethnic origins, culture and language have often been the basis for this kind of initiative. Asian communities in Britain would furnish many examples of this sort.

Where this kind of pattern develops on a more ambitious scale on behalf of a larger residential community it becomes a different kind of project for which there is no generally accepted name: a "community action project" it might be called. The Craigmillar Festival Society in Edinburgh was one of the first projects of this sort in Britain. In Australia, The Brotherhood of St. Lawrence, which began in Melbourne between the wars, has many of the same features. There are many other examples in the United States, in Spain, in France and elsewhere.

The single-purpose groups

What are the characteristic strengths and weaknesses of these projects? I will start with the more specialised, single-purpose groups which are much the most common.

Community-based services of this kind can do some urgently needed things which the state's services are not empowered to do and private enterprise is unable or unwilling to do – like setting up credit unions in impoverished communities where the alternatives are the illicit money lenders and the "heavies" who police their territory, the grocery vans whose drivers take child benefit books in return for credit at high rates of interest, the exploitative clothing clubs – and unpaid rent and fuel bills. Other single-purpose projects – like Glasgow's housing management co-operatives – do not create a new service, but provide a better one, more accountable to its users, than the state was able to offer. The Ballymun Job Centre Co-operative in Dublin, set up by people living on a remote housing estate, has created jobs by raising funds for local projects, has surveyed all the estate's residents and recorded the skills available, and has persuaded employers operating down town to come out and recruit workers from the estate.

It could be argued that if the state or the private sector are failing, it would be better to make them more effective than to compel poor people, in the few neighbourhoods capable of doing that, to go to the trouble of creating community-based alternatives. The state may be content with a strategy which keeps potential rebels docile by making them work flat out to keep a community business going. But should we accept that?

A sceptical question must always be asked about the need for community-based forms of service. It should not be assumed too readily that they offer the only solution for defects in more conventional services, public or private. That would be to absolve too easily the public service professions and the entrepreneurs whose authoritarian or profit motivated styles have sometimes compelled people to do their own thing when they would have preferred to rely on conventional services if only they would operate in more responsive, "user friendly" ways.

Meanwhile these single-purpose projects have some fundamental limitations of their own. They are best at meeting the needs of people who live together in one area – the residents of a particular housing estate, for example. They may be less good at mobilising a group dispersed throughout the country – gays or lesbians, for example.

These groups can become very conservative. Having argued and suffered together for years through the long meetings required to get their projects going, they create strong personal bonds and a power structure which may exclude newcomers with new ideas. The women who frequently played leading roles in the early, heroic years tend to be replaced by men experienced in committee procedures. A new kind of bureaucracy may take shape.

The same tendencies have been noted by leaders of the "woman church" and liberation theology movements who are well aware that, to survive, the radical group breaking away from the institutional Church cannot avoid becoming institutionalised in its turn.

This kind of local conservatism may restrict the range of customers a community-based group is prepared to serve. The selection procedures for tenants devised by housing management co-operatives in Glasgow would not recruit blacks, ex-prisoners, addicts or other stigmatised people unless they already had friends or relatives in the co-operative. It was the members of local community groups in deprived suburbs of Belfast and Dublin who mobilised with ugly threats of violence to drive travelling people out of their neighbourhoods.

But it was other local people, let it be remembered, who in some of these areas stood by the travellers and insisted that more civilised solutions be found. We should not conclude that the community-based approach cannot work. And we must remember that more conventional bureaucratic systems do not have a better record of playing fair with people who tend to get excluded on racist, sexist and other grounds.

All the same, the limitations of the single-purpose community groups should be recognised. Although they undoubtedly make bits of the world into better places, they are not going to change the world in any fundamental way. They cannot weigh up economic and social priorities in any general sense because they have only one priority – the particular job they set out to do. They cannot, single-handedly, bring the outcast and deprived into the mainstream of society. The state and the political parties, which for better or worse do have these responsibilities and have to operate on a larger scale, still have central roles, however extensive the community-based alternatives to conventional services may become.

Community action

Realism about the limitations of the specialist, single-purpose groups must prompt us to ask whether the more ambitious community action projects offer hope of a bolder shift towards open, accountable, egalitarian democracy. In parts of Northern Ireland it looked for a while as if that might be happening. In 1972, when disturbances in Belfast led to the temporary collapse of public services and thousands of people were compelled by fear to move out of mixed areas into communities of their own faith, local groups took over many of the functions of government. They erected barriers at the entrances to their neighbourhoods and policed them for 24 hours a day. They allocated houses to the homeless, and provided relief for people who had lost all they possessed. They set up taxi services. If they had a bakery within their territory but no dairy, they bartered bread for milk with other community groups and distributed these things to the families in need of them. But those were heroic days and special circumstances. What has happened since – there and in the rest of the British Isles?

Some community action groups operate on an impressive scale – at least for a while. The Pleck Community Council in Walsall and its associated enterprises have set up projects which provide gardening services, deliver milk, manage housing, run a boxing club, and many other things. The excellent play, which was the Easterhouse Festival Society's first major project, was written, produced and acted by local people, and gained a prize in the Edinburgh Festival Fringe. Later, EFS created the biggest outdoor mosaic in Europe – a beautiful and technically expert work of art which is about the only object on this huge estate which can be looked at with unmixed enjoyment. The Flax Trust in West Belfast has set up work spaces, training schemes, welfare services and created a large number of jobs. Many other examples of this sort could be given.

Such projects have taken initiatives which neither the public nor the private sector would have contemplated. Celebration through drama, music and art have been a recurring theme in community action, producing performances of vivid quality which assert the identity and history of the neighbourhood, and create links for it with the outside world. In places where examples of excellence are scarce and people often feel isolated and forgotten, those are very important achievements.

Some groups have made a fairly sophisticated analysis of their community's expenditure and skills, and set about creating enterprises which will use these skills to substitute for services brought in from elsewhere. When raising funds to build community centres, youth clubs, landscaped play areas and other things, some groups – Barrowfield in Glasgow is one of them – have successfully insisted that the jobs which those funds create come to their community. For black people – in Broadwater Farm and the Stonebridge Bus Garage, for example – that has brought opportunities to gain skills and set up enterprises which will enable them to compete in the wider world.

These groups are breaking out of the social isolation in which poor communities are often imprisoned. They are also bridging the gaps between economic and social policy, between physical and human development, and surmounting administrative barriers which cripple the state's services. Community action projects have often been more creative and adaptable than any bureaucracy could be.

Most important for the activists themselves has been the transforming experience these projects have given them. They have learnt capacities for leadership, gained the confidence to deal decisively with politicians, officials and professionals of all sorts, and demolished the myths of credentialism – the idea that you cannot do anything until you are labelled as officially qualified for the job. Their political clout can be formidable.

But a heavy price has been paid for these achievements. Community action projects typically have a turbulent history: internal and external conflicts and betrayals, threatened bankruptcy and allegations of fraud are commonplace. Leaders who stay the course may become unattractively hardened politicians. The characteristic styles of community action are spontaneous, emotionally direct, contentious, charismatic. They are entirely different from the bureaucratic routines which help people working in more conventional organisations to separate their personal from their professional lives, to argue without quarreling, to control the demands of their work with the help of the annual and monthly rhythms of budgets, committee meetings and holidays, and to get home at reasonably predictable times. It is not surprising that community activists tend to burn out fast.

The marks of success

These are the recurring patterns to be found in the more successful projects.

[1] They have *charismatic, committed leaders*. One will do, but often there will be several. Lacking the rituals which legitimise more conventional kinds of leadership, they have to establish their claim to power by sheer force of personality. They must also be deeply committed to the communities in which they operate. Professional community workers, like others in the public services, gain promotion and move on. The successful activists with local roots stay, working for nothing or for a pittance, and declining the well paid jobs which other places are apt to offer them as their achievements come to be recognised.

[2] People are not born with the capacity for collective action – the conviction that they and their neighbours can get together, challenge established authority, and change things. It has to be

110

learnt. Key members of the group usually have some *tradition of collective action* to draw on. But it may be derived from many different sources. Among those whom I have met it came from trade unionism, the revolutionary Labour movement, or a father who fought in Spain; from shared Caribbean or Asian origins and the experience of migration to a new and sometimes hostile country; from Republican or Protestant loyalties (as in the Ulster projects); or from religious conviction which may be a protestant one (as in Caribbean groups) or a Catholic one (alive in parts of Scotland as well as Ireland, north and south – sometimes with the support of priests and ministers, sometimes despite their opposition).

The education provided by social movements is profoundly important, and it can be transmitted from one generation to the next. These movements teach more than the techniques of collective action; they teach generous loyalties, capacities for self sacrifice, scepticism about established authority, and the ability to handle conflict. They keep alive the idea that the human race is making a journey together, guided by far reaching convictions and sustained by comradeship.

[3] Charismatic leadership is not enough by itself. Some *paid staff* are needed. Even one person can make a big difference. The mobilised community, confronting an assault upon its interests, can be very effective. Stopping things is relatively easy. But the long haul required to make things happen is much harder. As the drive for more positive action begins, there will be delays, complications and long periods of boredom – while raising funds, applying for planning permission, negotiating with politicians and public service unions. The impetus will be lost unless someone is paid to remember what's happening, to keep the files, to answer the telephone, and work patiently towards the group's goals.

[4] If paid workers are to have sufficient security to stick at the job for a while, there must be *a flow of funds* to pay them. The temptation is to rely on temporary funding, provided by central government for job creation or social innovation projects which will be snatched away just as the group begins to take off. So some more reliable flow of cash must be found.

[5] That usually calls for *a building* of some sort, or several buildings – an asset which can be rented out over the longer term, or just for meetings and other activities. A building can also be used as collateral for the loans required to start up new enterprises. And the conversion and maintenance of it may bring further

111

Making our future

grants, jobs and training opportunities to the community. If it achieves what its creators hope for, the Stonebridge Bus Garage will be one of the most dramatic examples of this kind. But there are many more. Housing co-operatives – like Calvay in Glasgow, which is aiming to set up shops and workshops and take over a nearby school for community activities – need not confine their work to the modernisation and management of their housing.

[6] To acquire staff and convert buildings means negotiating loans, grants and contracts, and securing permissions and approvals of many kinds. All that calls for skill, tact and staying power – and friends at court. The leaders of every successful community action project owe a good deal to one or two *friendly officials* who in their early days explained the bureaucracy to them (its committees, its annual financial cycle, how to fill in application forms) and helped them gain access to the corridors of power (explaining how to approach charitable trusts for funds, how to get a meeting with a Minister or the convener of a key committee, and what to say when they got there).

[7] But official friends, however powerful, are not enough. The leaders of a successful community action project have to establish a *working relationship with local politicians*, both to gain their support when it is needed, and to fight off take-over bids – for the politicians always attempt to gain as much credit as they can for themselves from successful projects. The activists must retain their independence; and that will only be achieved if they earn it by putting down roots within the community which make them a political force in their own right. That may be achieved through good welfare rights work and by gaining the ear of local newspapers and radio stations, and through their capacity to provide authentic information about what's going on in the area. A group which has achieved those things can establish sound relations with the politicians, based on recognition that each needs, but neither can exploit, the other.

[8] Their backers in the public authorities and the charitable foundations often press the leaders of community action projects to claim that they represent the communities they serve. They feel more comfortable giving funds to a group which can be described as "representative". The claim is easily made, for in terms of race, class and gender the group are usually more representative of their community (in the sense of resembling them more closely) than the local council or the trustees of a charity; and their activities

112

are usually conducted in a more public fashion. So some groups do claim to speak, not only for their project but for their "community". But later, when things go wrong – as, to some degree, they always will – their backers will be among the first to say that the group are "not really representative".

Shrewder groups refuse to claim that they represent anyone but those involved in their project. They try instead to *operate in an accountable fashion* – accountable to their members and neighbours, the people whom they serve, and those who give them money. Different forms and procedures of accountability have to be developed for these different purposes. Meanwhile they leave to democratically elected assemblies the job of representing people.

[9]   *Financial accountability* is particularly important. It is predictable that when money is given to impoverished groups their leaders will before long be accused of fraud – often by their own neighbours. The accusation is usually false, but must be answered. Thus, besides developing fairly thick skins, the group must devise regular procedures for demonstrating to themselves and to outsiders how their money is being spent, month by month as well as year by year. In Ulster, where it is often alleged that public funds find their way to paramilitaries, people have devised particularly effective accounting procedures of this sort.

[10]   Success often brings disillusionment, a falling off in public support, and growing criticism from local people whose expectations have in some way been disappointed. Even the most extensive project can usually employ only a handful of the people who would have liked to get a job in it. A housing co-operative, once it has let all the houses it produces and landscaped the surrounding spaces, has little more to offer except the hard grind of managing the property. So people stop coming to meetings. The projects which surmount these hazards best are those which *welcome newcomers and encourage them to launch new projects* – semi-independent offshoots of the original enterprise.

These are perhaps the ten commandments for community activists suggested by the experience of some of the most successful of them.

Lessons for civic leaders

Most community projects need a delicate combination of official support and political independence. To tie them too closely to the state restricts their capacity to do new things in new ways, and makes it likely that they will be destroyed if the parties controlling the state change (as Liverpool voluntary organisations know to their cost). But it will be easier to give community-based projects the elbow room they need if public authorities and charitable foundations sort out with them before contracts are signed a number of problems which are bound to arise.

Financial accountability, for example, may not be best assured by bringing in a qualified, white, male manager or accountant. It may be that the qualified people willing to work in what their own professional colleagues would regard as rather eccentric, underpaid jobs are not the ablest or most honest members of their professions. Some of the more serious disasters have arisen from such appointments. So teaching the local activists, whenever possible, to do their own accounting and management will often be a wiser strategy. But that will not happen unless it is properly planned and budgeted for in advance.

Many other problems can be foreseen and sorted out before they arise. When projects recruit staff and appoint contractors, are the selection of people with local knowledge and credibility, and the development of skills and entrepreneurial capacity within the local community to be among the main aims? Or would the appointment of the project leaders' friends and neighbours be regarded as scandalous nepotism?

If the group is to allocate scarce resources – houses, for example – are they expected to do that in ways which stabilise and strengthen the local community (by enabling local youngsters to find a home near their parents, for example); or in ways which meet the most urgent needs to be found throughout the city?

If leading members of the project are asked to serve on committees advising Ministers or to advise contractors bidding for work associated with similar projects elsewhere, should they be paid for that? And if so, does that money go to them or to the project? If they are living on social security payments will they be allowed to accept *any* payment? If some of them want to take courses and look for salaried jobs doing the kind of work they have been doing for nothing, would that be a betrayal of their

comrades, or is it one of the aims of the whole movement?
Every one of these questions has been a subject of fierce
argument. Any of the answers proposed might be right; but the
questions will be more constructively handled if they are discussed
in advance, and not left like unexploded mines to be stepped on
later.

Fresh thought will be needed about many other questions too.
Established institutions, statutory and voluntary, are accustomed
to send their staff on training courses and to professional
conferences. But if local activists are to have similar opportunities,
different arrangements will have to be made. Money must be
found for their travel and subsistence; different kinds of training
will be needed; and conferences must meet at different times of the
day and the week, make provision for the care of young children
while their parents are engaged in these activities, and be
organised in quite different ways.

In future, professional staff will more frequently move back
and forth in the course of their careers between established
statutory and voluntary organisations, the private sector and
community-based projects, and will be better equipped for their
jobs by this varied experience. A whole career spent in one service
within one type of central or local government department will
become much less common than it used to be. To make those
transitions easier will call for fresh thought about pension schemes,
promotion procedures and related trade union agreements.

Conclusions

What are the main conclusions to which this chapter leads? First,
it is clear that community-based action, initiated "from the bottom
upwards", has made a dent in people's lives and in the
conventional bureaucratic and commercial systems. Things have
been achieved which neither the state nor the market were ever
likely to bring about. The activists' lives have often been changed.
So, too, have the outlook and methods of other people who have
worked most closely with them. My colleague, a professor in the
medical school, who insists that his students should talk about
"complementary medicine", not "alternative medicine", has been
changed in this way. The Scottish firm of landscape architects and
engineers who include in their bids a sum for training local

115

resident groups to set up the enterprises which will enable the main contractor to subcontract work to them – they too have been changed.

But community-based enterprises are not going to supplant the state or private enterprise. Even in Northern Ireland, where they had the best chance of doing so, all three sources of initiative are needed, and work best when the state gives a generous and consistent lead. Successful community-based action calls for continuing, patient advice and support from within the bureaucracy – preferably with some backing from the charitable foundations which helps community projects to retain their independence. (In Northern Ireland, which lacks such foundations, the state was wise enough to set one up – the Northern Ireland Voluntary Trust. In the Republic, the Combat Poverty Agency does some of the same things.)

Even with that kind of support, community action will not develop everywhere. The capacity for it is nurtured by social movements of various kinds – movements not confined to the revolutionary working class. Race, religion, gender and other factors also play a part, giving people the capacity to mobilise and work together, and the confidence to challenge authority. But, while every society and generation seem to find their own ways of keeping that flame alight, we cannot assume it will burn in every neighbourhood all the time. So community action will always be patchy.

Where these initiatives take off, the eternal problems of government still have to be solved. Establishing legitimate authority, providing for the succession of new leaders when the old leaders are discarded, distinguishing public from private money and accounting for public spending, giving the people rights which they can rely on, arranging appeals to an independent authority for customers and staff who believe they have been unfairly treated, keeping the public informed about what those in authority are doing – all this still has to be done. Initially at least, community-based action tends to be better at some of these things (like keeping the people informed) and worse at others (like providing for the succession). But it has no special magic for surmounting these problems.

The activists are fallible human beings, and they don't walk on water. Charles Manson, whose "family" killed Sharon Tate, led a community of sorts. The Bradford Muslims, who have called for the death of Salman Rushdie, speak for a community. I have seen the telephone box in a Belfast back street to which delinquent youngsters are sent to ring for an ambulance before they are knee-capped – youngsters called out of their homes for punishment without trial by men who claim to represent their community.

The difficult questions posed by these examples can only be answered within the framework of larger communities and their more broadly-based power structures. Those are among the themes of the next chapter.

As people work out new ways of solving the old problems, they begin to look more and more like the thing they originally rebelled against; just as heretics, when they get organised, look more and more like an institutional Church. Thus the aim of community activists should not be to supplant the state or private enterprise, but to shove both in directions which they would not otherwise take, to convey to the world an authentic, irreverent, "bottom-up" view of the workings of power, and to gain a hearing – and a better life – for people and places that would otherwise be forgotten. As a Hungarian friend of mine said, "It is only failed revolutions that succeed".

QUESTIONS

1 List some of the things which you would hope public officials would learn from working closely with community activists. What should the activists learn from officials?

2 The conclusions of this chapter have been drawn mainly from studies of community action by groups concentrated in particular neighbour-hoods. What more – or what different things – must be said when considering the needs of people not concentrated in this way? Women for example? Or gay men?

3 Your local authority's housing committee, encouraged by a mental health pressure group, is insisting that the next house to be let in a poverty-stricken neighbourhood, where many families are struggling to get by, should go to a difficult, mentally deranged person. The residents' action group object and threaten to blockade the house. You have been asked to arbitrate between them. How would you try to help?

4 You are the Director of Education for a large city and your committee has instructed you to involve the public more effectively in planning

117

new developments, and to pay particular attention to groups gaining least benefit from your services. Your first initiatives gain an immediate response from the most highly educated people and the leafier suburbs. But elsewhere there is apathy. You fear that a more participative style of administration will only divert yet more of your scarce resources to those who have least need of them. What would you do?

5 You are a government Minister in a strife-torn society where the clergy are pressing you for recognition and funds which will give them leadership of community action in poor areas which may otherwise be taken over by the local gunmen. But democracy, power sharing and accountability to local people are not what their Church is most famous for. How would you respond?

6 Do we have to accept that there will always be severely deprived communities in big cities? This is one of the questions we must turn to in the next chapter.

7 | The civic agenda

Why places matter

I have recently been working in a public housing estate which is about the most impoverished quarter of the prosperous city in which it stands. Many of the four thousand people who live there are unemployed. Many got a house there because they and their partners broke up, or they were coming out of mental hospital or prison, and this is where a spare flat can always be found. Large numbers of youngsters leave the secondary school with no job to go to; the police report high rates of petty crime. Meanwhile the housing managers try to chase up rent arrears. Yet investment has been poured into this city over many years, and unemployment rates are well below the nation's averages. If a rising tide *did* lift all boats, everyone here would be prospering.

But all is not gloom. The public authorities, who run everything in this neighbourhood, are concerned about its people and want to give them a voice in planning for its future. As a result of their efforts there is an excellent youth project, funded through the Region's Education Department and largely run by local volunteers. There is a family project, funded through the Social Work Department, with play equipment for children, a welfare rights worker, a small library, a well-equipped darkroom for photographers, computers for those who want to learn how to use the new technologies, and much else. There is also an expensive new community centre, built by the District Housing Department, which – like the other projects – is run by a committee of local people. And there are several more projects of similar kinds. Which all sounds fine.

But the youth club is not allowed to use the equipment in the family project because its committee does not approve of teenagers. And the older people who are in charge of the community centre plan to hold carpet bowls and bingo sessions there and are reluctant to let youngsters or families in. The social workers do not visit the youth project, backed by the Education Department – although many families go there for advice and support in times of trouble. The teachers are unaware of the expensive learning resources lying idle in the family centre, backed by the Social Work Department. And when innocent researchers like me suggest that those who launched these initiatives should meet with local residents and get their act together on behalf of all who live in this estate, we are told that they are all "community based". So noone can intrude on them. And teachers, social workers and housing managers find it difficult to work together. And the Region and the District are controlled by different political parties.

This is an absolutely normal situation. A commitment to work with poor communities and give them a voice only makes sense if it is set within a larger framework capable of mobilising people's concerns for a wider community of some kind. The potentially conflicting demands of smaller groups must be reconciled by creative political leaders responsible to a larger public. Professional staff, no matter how talented they may be, cannot do that unaided. Indeed, professional cultures and practices are often the most narrowly belligerent of the lot.

Meanwhile, in some of the richest places in the world, there are city centres where commercial developers have created enchanting environments, with shops at ground level, offices upstairs and penthouse flats on top. In the centre of these precincts stand instant trees, brought in from the most expensive nurseries; and overhead you can see the sky. To walk through them is like taking a little holiday. But the less respected citizens have been excluded from these places; sometimes by social pressures; sometimes by uniformed guards. Those excluded then roam the increasingly bleak and violent streets and subways, on which the new, skyscraping developments turn a repellent backside of loading bays, refuse chutes and guarded entrances.

Out in the leafier suburbs, other developers are building what they used to call "garden villages" or "new towns". From these, again, the poor are usually excluded.

Where then do the poor go? In Britain that question usually takes us back to the less attractive public housing estates. I am at the moment working in one of the worst in England. For years, no-one with any choice about where they live has been prepared to go there. Flats stand in monstrous blocks. In some of these, one-third of the flats are empty, while many of the others are occupied by squatters. Women are afraid to live here, so most of the residents are men. Nearly half move on in the course of a year. Down the road there is the largest drug dealing market in the north of England, bringing with it the constant threat of violence. Break-ins, burglaries and muggings are common; rape and other brutalities are more frequent than elsewhere. Graffiti are daubed all over the place. Staff of the public services seem to have given up: repairs are not done; rubbish is left uncollected; letters are not delivered. "This", said one of the residents, "is the estate where the rotweilers walk in pairs".

This is the kind of place often found not far from the exclusive neighbourhoods created by the prospering market. Compelled to cope as best they can here, people protect themselves in ways which make life worse for everyone. Because the whole estate is so intimidating, women and old people rarely go out alone in the evenings. Indeed, many of them rarely go out at all. Young children are not allowed to play out of doors. Steel panels, nailed by the Housing Department to doors and windows to keep thieves out when flats are empty, are often left in place by the new tenants because they feel safer that way – even though it means living in the dark. You might be in the frontier streets of Belfast or Beirut. "Community" is not a word that means much here. Individualism has triumphed.

Once again, only civic leadership on a larger scale can put things right. Flats of intolerable design must be pulled down or transformed. Opportunities must be opened up for people who have been virtually excluded from the life of their city. Public services must be made accountable to their customers. Commercial services must be brought in. There are no banks, no building societies and few shops. Even taxis are reluctant to enter the estate. A sense of community must be rebuilt. The tenants on this estate are in fact battling to achieve these things; but they cannot do it by themselves.

If we are concerned about human rights and opportunities, the town is the main arena in which we must act. Ministers and their civil servants who live in capital cities often find it difficult to take other towns seriously. But each is a different place, offering different opportunities. The chances of getting a decent house or job, of catching bronchitis or dying of cancer, of getting a proper education for your children – all these vary enormously from place to place. Even when the influences of social class, family size and many other factors which are known to affect attainment have been excluded, ten-year-olds in different types of British town differ by a year or more in their average reading ages and in their knowledge of mathematics. And most of these differences between towns are growing larger, not smaller.

Differences between villages are just as important. I am using the word "town" as short-hand for "human settlement", and am not concerned only with the urban world. Nevertheless, when our precariously thin veneer of civilisation breaks down and the anger brewing in an increasingly unfair society bursts out in violence on the streets (as it has done in Britain and will do again) it is in the big, old cities that trouble begins. This is where ideas of community and citizenship and the credibility of government itself are being tested – tested sometimes to destruction.

The next section of this chapter explains the causes and character of the crisis that afflicts many cities in countries like Britain, and shows how inadequate our urban policies have been. After that I outline a progressive response to these problems. Then, as in previous chapters, I sharpen that outline by defining its enemies. Finally I ask what the "just" or "equal" city might look like, and draw some general conclusions.

The urban crisis

"Crisis" is an over-used word. But in this case it is justified. Drastic changes are taking place in the industrial systems of all the rich countries. Old industries decline as they are succeeded by new ones which rely on machines that replace labour and demand new skills. Anyone who has seen an old steel works, textile mill or coal mine and their modernised successors will know what that means. Whether the works close or are modernised, there will be a drastic decline in the numbers employed and big changes in the skills needed.

Major economic changes have happened before. But they now happen much faster. It took more than a century for Britain's agricultural labour force to be halved by increasing productivity and foreign competition, but only fourteen years for Britain's manufacturing industries to shed one-third of their labour without loss of output. And this is only the beginning. The new technology is now spreading into office work and service industries that hitherto provided a safety net for many families whose working members were squeezed out of manufacturing jobs. After 1992 and the creation of a single European market, the wheels of change will run faster still.

In the past, we took much of the benefit of higher productivity in the form of leisure and training which were achieved by reducing people's working lives – postponing entry to the labour force through longer education, reducing working hours, increasing weekly and annual holidays, and giving people pensions which enabled them to retire earlier. All of this took time, but time was available. Then, in every generation, we started wars which quickly burnt up surplus goods and people and led to a whole generation of reconstruction.

Despite the adjustment provided in these ways, economic development was enormously costly in human suffering, political turmoil and the destruction of communities. Historians still argue over the benefits, if any, conferred on working people by the industrial revolution.

Now we are having to cope with much more rapid economic and social changes in a world in which we can no longer risk a war. The industries, the skills and the people squeezed out by change are heavily concentrated in the older cities in which their predecessors were previously most successful: the boom towns of the late Victorian years.

The results are familiar: closed factories, growing numbers of people with little training or obsolete skills who have been out of work for long periods, low rates of technical innovation, few new enterprises starting up, more people taking to crime or seeking escape through drugs and alcohol, and an outflow of the younger and more highly skilled workers who leave behind a growing concentration of the elderly, the sick, the lone parents and others with nowhere else to go. Such cities are to be found in most advanced economies.

"The inner city" was the term coined to describe these areas. But there are jobs, pubs and life of many kinds in the inner parts of our towns, grotty though they may be. The worst poverty, the bleakest exclusion, are found in the big housing estates built –

often on the edge of town – as dormitories for the families whose breadwinners were expected to work in the factories that closed.

Public policies

For many years British governments of both parties tried with subsidies and through controls on the use of land to encourage development in the failing regions of the country. And they had some success in slowing down the rate of decay and attracting new enterprises – though nowhere near enough to stem the tide of economic decline. After 1979 "regional policies" were abandoned, and drastic cuts were made in the flow of central funds to local authorities – particularly the authorities responsible for the most severely stricken cities. Since then, new initiatives have been taken to set up Enterprise Zones, Task Forces and Urban Development Corporations, and to provide Urban Development Grants and Employment Allowances. There is no need to explain precisely what all this formidable machinery means. It has brought far less funds to the cities concerned than were taken away by cuts in rate support grant. The 60,000 jobs which the government claims to have created over six years in England by these measures probably amount to a net increase of half this amount when account is taken of other jobs replaced or transferred as a result of these initiatives. Meanwhile unemployment in the same cities rose by over 160,000 to 1.2 million during the same period, leaving them with a larger share of the nation's unemployed than they started with.

This failure is not surprising. The government's initiatives were designed to improve buildings and their surrounding urban environment and to subsidise enterprises prepared to invest in these places. They were not designed to improve workers' skills or help the long-term unemployed. Employers have not been obliged to recruit local labour, to subcontract work to local enterprises, or to hire people who have been out of work for a long time. Urban Development Corporations have not been expected to work closely with local communities: indeed, some have been at war with their representatives.

In England, the government's main aims seem to have been to brush aside local civic leaders, to take over parts of their physical and administrative territory temporarily, and to achieve some visible impact which will bring credit to Ministers – not to develop a sustained, comprehensive, city-wide response to the urban crisis. Scotland, through the Scottish Development Agency, has done a good deal better.

The British government's background assumption has been that the market, freed from controls, will gradually spread the booming growth to be seen in parts of London's economy to all corners of the country. But finance capital, not manufacturing capital, is the dominant influence in London's growth, and its directors are far more concerned about the short-term gains to be made by shuffling money around the world than about the long-term future of Liverpool, Newcastle or Glasgow. As the cost of land and premises increases, many firms are indeed leaving London; but they don't go far: 80 per cent of them come to rest within about 80 miles of London. Meanwhile much the most powerful government influences upon regional and urban development have been wielded, not through the programmes I have listed, but through increased spending on defence and aerospace technology, most of which goes to prosperous southern areas around and between London and Bristol.

Local government often did little better than central government. Slowly, however, by creating Enterprise Boards and support services of various kinds, and trying to work more closely with the people living in stricken areas, some local authorities are beginning to address the real problems of their cities. Although the jobs they have created or saved have not transformed these cities, they have generally been achieved at much lower cost than those claimed by central government. And because civic leaders are accountable to their own citizens they have wisely laid more emphasis on preserving jobs (which are more likely to be held by the less skilled) than on creating new ones (which tend to go to more skilled people, often recruited from elsewhere).

The crisis I have described is national and ultimately worldwide in its scope and origins. It makes its most vivid impact in parts of the older, industrial cities, but its effects are to be seen in villages and small towns too: alongside closed pits in West Virginia or steelworks in Northern France or South Wales, for example. Inevitably it afflicts the more obsolete, the less innovative, parts of an economy, and those furthest from the power centres of multinational enterprise. These changes are not some disease that originates in the places or among the people that suffer most; yet the language used to describe what happens – the talk about "the urban crisis", "the inner city" and "the underclass" – encourages people to believe that those who live in these places are the problem, not merely its victims.

A *progressive response*

If you want to know what should be done about depressed cities and impoverished neighbourhoods, start with the people who live in them and listen carefully to what they say – respecting and tolerating the anger that is often the first response of the oppressed.

Jobs are what most people think of first. But footholds on the jobs ladder must be matched by footholds on supporting ladders of opportunity for education and training, for housing, and for public and commercial services.

These people know that a town is not just a labour market. If success in school compels youngsters to leave home because there are so few jobs nearby for qualified people; if families who want to buy, or to rent, a decent house at a price they can afford have to move elsewhere because the kind of home they want is not available here; if there are no opportunities to go to a concert, a theatre or a good football game, or to play in one, then talent will be lost to other towns, skills will be under-used, the motivation to succeed will be eroded, and ambitious young families from other places will not be prepared to come and throw in their lot with this community. A successful community must offer ladders of opportunity in every field of activity – every sector of the economy.

A community's development will be stunted by discontinuities in these ladders – gaps in the rungs which noone can jump – and by disjunctions between them – footholds on one ladder which are too far from others on neighbouring ladders of opportunity. To get things right we have to think of all these dimensions of a city's life and make sure that they develop in balance with each other. Listening to the people will make it easier to remember that.

That is why people in deprived neighbourhoods demand action on many other things besides jobs – to clear the rubbish away, demolish derelict buildings, and remove the young glue sniffers who haunt them. They will be right to do so. Noone will

126

invest energy or money in places which look so unloved. However, businesses and bureaucracies are not good at dealing with multi-faceted problems. They are programmed to tackle specific tasks: to train workers for jobs already available, or to build shops where a demand for them can be guaranteed, not to worry about communities with no jobs and no money to spend. They build houses where they can be quickly let or sold, and do not see house building as being also an opportunity for stabilising a community, improving skills and creating jobs. Many of these organisations – public and private alike – have little reason to think in any other way. Indeed, they rely on pools of unemployed labour, derelict land, empty houses – all the resources lying idle in deprived neighbourhoods – which they can draw in and cast off according to the fluctuating needs of their own operations.

Meanwhile, in the poorest neighbourhoods, many of the people will not be much interested in paid work, at least for the time being. They are old, or sick, or disabled, or looking after young children single-handed. For them, an effective welfare rights service will be more useful, bringing them pensions, disability benefits, family benefits, housing benefits, free bus passes, free school meals, free prescriptions – all of it money to which they are legally entitled but which they often fail to get. When these people spend the money, this also makes it a little easier to keep a shop, an electrician, a pub or a coal merchant going in their neighbourhood. People can be trained and supported to run their own welfare rights services, instead of relying on professional experts who may be efficient, but do nothing to give them back the power which is, most fundamentally, what they lack.

Such local initiatives must be set within a city-wide strategy designed to deal with at least three different kinds of neighbourhood:

☐ The city centre, where – on the unfashionable sides of town – there will often be decaying warehouses, railway sidings and docks.

☐ The old inner city, once packed with industrial premises and landlords' housing – a territory now patched with small municipal estates, and often carved up by ring roads – some half finished and then abandoned.

☐ The less popular neighbourhoods of the big public housing

127

estates, some built in inner areas, but most of them standing on the less accessible fringes of the town.

If anything is to be achieved, the public and the private sectors will have to collaborate closely in these places, working with a joint commitment to get their city moving in the right directions. That will call for sustained, consistent and expensive public policies to convince private investors that civic leaders are determined to bring about changes which they can participate in and profit from.

Celebration

I will say more about the private sector later. But first I want to stress the importance of "the arts". Some of the most effective investments made by public authorities in Glasgow during recent years have been in galleries, theatres, music, museums and a garden festival. Together, these things have helped to give citizens confidence in their heritage, to attract creative people, to convince those who can choose where they live that this is a good place to be. They also bring in huge numbers of tourists. Other cities are following the same path.

Support for the arts has sometimes been condemned as élitist – as indeed it can be. But it need not be like that. Glasgow made a systematic attempt to involve school children, ethnic minorities and the mentally and physically handicapped in the programme with which it celebrated its year as "cultural city of Europe". The arts are often thought of as icing on the cake – to be added to an urban renewal scheme in the hope that the Gulbenkian Foundation, the Arts Council or some other fairy godmother may be induced to pay for them. But it is precisely among people who have lost their industries, skills and houses, and been devastated by slum clearance, factory closures or road building schemes, that memories of who they were and still are can be most precious. Those who can readily take a taxi to the Royal Academy between London appointments do not think of the arts in this way. They take their culture and the subsidies which support it for granted, unaware of the huge privileges they enjoy.

Springburn, where the finest steam locomotives in the world were once built, has become a sprawling, half destroyed, half rebuilt, non-place. In the midst of this mess a museum has been opened, partly run by local people who have collected relics of every aspect of their history and involved their own youngsters in creating exhibitions (most recently celebrating, and lamenting, "teenage" as they experience it today). It also has a resident artist who invites visitors to come back and work with her in the evenings; and some of them do.

If a choice has to be made, these celebrations are just as important as, and far cheaper than, the improvements to buildings and landscape which public authorities are happier to pay for.

Community business

Local participation is just as important in other fields. If damp, cold houses need new heating systems and better insulation, if a security service is needed to patrol the neighbourhood and keep it safe, if the graffiti are to be cleaned off the walls and stairways, and derelict lots are to be planted with grass and trees which will later have to be cared for, then local people must be offered this work whenever possible – not just by hiring a few of them as unskilled labourers, but by helping them to set up their own enterprises, subcontracting work to them, and encouraging them later to bid for contracts elsewhere in the city.

In some cities these things are happening already, but only where people are offered some training, and, with the support of local politicians, gain a seat at the decision making meetings. Then contractors take them seriously, for they know there will be further jobs in the pipeline for which they will be bidding in future. No longer do they send in a hard-hatted army to clean things up and drive away again in big trucks. They take time and trouble to help local people set up their own enterprises, subcontract work to them – and two years later the improvements they have made are still a well maintained advertisement for their firm, not vandalised to destruction.

The public services – providing education, parks and recreation for example – need to learn similar lessons. If a new education or recreation centre, a new park, swimming pool or library, are to be set up in deprived neighbourhoods, local people must be involved from the start. Too often, when the bureaucrats capture funds from central or local government or from Brussels by offering to do something for such areas, they charge fees for entry or provide a menu of exhibits and activities which exclude the deprived. The cars standing in their car parks show only too clearly what kind of customers they are catering for.

The larger scale

The renewal of cities stricken by economic change cannot be brought about without help from the nation at large. That will call for financial support given on terms which oblige local political leaders to seek alliances with private and voluntary interests.

The example set by the Scottish Development Agency has a good deal to teach us. The Agency did not march into cities with the powers of an Urban Development Corporation which takes over chunks of the local authority's territory with authority to redevelop it. The SDA could only offer money, and negotiate a contract with local authorities, community groups and private enterprise to persuade them all to collaborate in renewing and regenerating towns or parts of them.

The private sector

Since private enterprises actually do most of the rebuilding which these cities require, it scarcely needs to be said that their role is an important one. But their managers too often look upon the city as no more than a place in which to make the money that enables them to enjoy a suburban life somewhere else.

If you operate on the scale of Marks and Spencer it is obvious that you should buy nearly all your goods from the country whose people are your customers. How can you sell the goods back to them if they are out of work? A prosperous high street depends on prosperous back streets.

It is not so widely understood that the same logic applies more loosely at a local scale to firms serving local markets. Businesses which appreciate the importance of a healthy urban environment can have a wide influence from which they, too, will benefit. When they want to recruit managers and technical staff the applicants will be concerned about the quality of the local schools and health services. They will be wondering whether their

130

children can walk the streets safely, and whether they will be able to park their cars without having the radios ripped out as soon as their backs are turned. The quality of life in the city where a business operates and the worldwide reputation of that city form a major part of that business's assets or liabilities.

In most British cities the numbers of people between the ages of 18 and 25 are going to fall by at least 20 per cent during the next few years. For an enterprise hoping to recruit more salesmen, technicians, nurses or secretaries the large numbers of teenagers now growing up on public housing estates with scant prospects of a decent job could be an important resource – but only if they are found, attracted and trained.

These things make a measurable difference. When the University of Liverpool, which stands on the edge of Toxteth – within sight of the riots that took place there – began to make a systematic attempt to involve itself in the city's life and problems, to help local schools, to buy from local people and to welcome more of them into its courses, its annual bill for broken windows was halved.

Every progressive manager is aware that a good business has responsibilities not only to its share holders but to all who hold a stake in its operations: its workers, suppliers, creditors, customers and neighbours. Businesses are stakeholders in the cities and towns where they operate. This is more widely recognised in some other countries. In many parts of the United States and Canada business leaders who do not contribute a significant percentage of their profits to projects which benefit the communities in which they operate would not be welcome at clubs and dinner tables around town.

However, community initiatives are likely to wither, and businesses to look for easier territories, unless the state gives a consistent, continuing lead, which shows it is determined to turn failing cities around. Only then will the other partners stop worrying about the risks of getting involved, and become concerned about the risks of *not* getting involved. The response takes time – but not an eternity. When public authorities set about renewing Glasgow's east end – then probably the biggest area of urban dereliction in Europe – they poured public funds into rebuilding houses, renewing the landscape and building small factories for about six years before the private sector began to build houses and factories. Then, when they turned to the city centre and next, to the peripheral housing estates, the same thing happened, but private developers responded sooner and more confidently.

To make this partnership really effective, all three of the partners – the public sector, the private sector and the local community – need to share a common sense of direction, a vision of the kind of city they want to create – which is broadly understood by a wider public. That will differ for each city, and it should do. Each is a different place. But there can be no continuing partnership unless the vision includes a determination to share and spread the opportunities the city offers more widely and more equally among all citizens. If cities grow increasingly unequal in the opportunities and living standards they offer – as British cities are now doing, whether we make comparisons between them or between different neighbourhoods within them – the alliance among the main partners will remain precariously liable to disintegrate.

The opposition

The argument for progressive urban policies sounds – I hope – too convincing to provoke much resistance; yet a lot of powerful people do resist it. There are people on the far Right who assert that the only "urban" policy which makes sense is to eliminate state interventions and controls, and let the market rip. Others on the far Left assert that all policies of a bourgeois democracy are little more than a conspiracy in the service of capitalism. The practical implications of both views are much the same. Britain's Conservative government, despite its rhetoric about freeing the people and rolling back the state, centralised power to a greater extent than any peace-time regime we have had, and deliberately destroyed local civic leadership.

City planning doesn't always work. Some attempts to plan have been useless or worse. But the idea that government in a modern state can simply "lift off" is an illusion. If official regional policies are abandoned, then the regional impact of defence expenditures, or other interventions such as the building of the channel tunnel and its associated rail routes, take over instead as powerful, if unofficial, "regional policies": policies, moreover, which flow with the economic tide and therefore tend to benefit the regions already favoured by that tide.

The idea that the main choice confronting us is whether to vote for the state or the market is about as sophisticated a piece of political analysis as that of George Orwell's sheep who, in *Animal Farm* chanted "Four legs good! Two legs bad!". Market forces must be respected and mobilised for humane purposes. That can only be done when the state gives sustained and coherent leadership, creating a framework within which the private sector can operate with confidence. The countries which have gone furthest to create a society which is both prosperous and equal, have done this not by nationalising the private sector, but by giving it a framework and a sense of direction within which to operate.

Meanwhile, there are still a few powerful people, particularly in the public sector and the big civil engineering companies, who see in tatty, poverty-stricken neighbourhoods a problem to be cleared away by the bulldozer. These people are the relics of the "heroic" days of urban planning. Some of our bleakest and poorest neighbourhoods were produced by their bulldozers and the wholesale rebuilding that followed. Wherever the poor and the powerless congregate, neglect and squalor will tend to reemerge; for investment, public as well as private, is withdrawn from such areas.

Some people have argued that within our cities technological advances are excluding a growing "underclass" of the least able people, who have been made unemployable by the increasing skills demanded of workers. That belief, for which no systematic evidence has been advanced, flies in the face of common knowledge. Baffling though it seemed at first sight, the word processor on which I am writing is much easier to use than the pen on which I once relied. Likewise the modern tractor driver has an easier job ploughing a field than the man who used to do it with a team of horses; and the coal miner pressing switches on a huge cutter and loader has a far easier task than his forbears who hewed and loaded with pick and shovel, lying on their sides in narrow coal seams. "User friendly" is the key phrase describing what we all expect, and generally get, from the new technology.

It may be the more complex "innards" of the new machines which encourage the delusion that they call not only for different skills but for much more sophisticated ones. Yet the service industries which have grown up to look after them make their maintenance as well as their operation easier. We used to tinker with our pens when they broke down, and I took the engine of my first car apart to "decoke" and reassemble it; but no-one expects me to take my word processor or the more complex engine of my present car apart.

If large numbers of people are left out of work, that is because noone thought it worth their while to train them, not because they are too dim to do the jobs available.

Conclusions

What would the "equal" or "just" city be like? It would hold a wide variety of people of different ages, classes, races and cultures. It would not be "equal" in the sense that everyone within it was just like everyone else. It would be clean and attractive; and opportunities for many different kinds of achievement would be plentiful and steadily expanding.

The potentially vulnerable groups – the families with several young children (particularly the lone parents), the pensioners (particularly those living on their own), the manual workers (particularly the unskilled) and the ethnic minorities would be doing well. A high proportion of them would own houses and cars.

Less vulnerable citizens – childless, white, highly qualified adults in the prime of life – would also be doing well, but would not be so far ahead of the average standards attained throughout the nation by their own groups as the vulnerable would be. There would be no more social segregation than those with least choice in the matter would prefer. And these idyllic conditions would be achieved without impoverishing other towns.

The 1981 Census, which provides crude evidence about many of these factors (but nothing on happiness or income, and little on health) suggests that this is not an impossible dream. The British towns where the manual workers, the unskilled, the lone parents and pensioners and the ethnic minorities do best tend to be the more prosperous, but less fashionable, suburbs around London and the Midlands towns, and some of the southern new towns.

Poole on the Dorset coast, and Hinckley and Bosworth on the western fringe of Leicester are examples of places where the vulnerable both do well by comparison with similar people in other towns, and do well by comparison with those in more privileged groups within their own town.

Several conclusions can be drawn from this evidence. The

places which treat their most vulnerable people best tend to be growing and prosperous: so if we care about these people we must take economic growth seriously. The privileged groups – the childless, the professionals and managers – also do well there; so all classes have a common interest in prosperity. But these more fortunate people do rather less well, relative to their own kind, than the manual workers do. Thus these are rather more equal places than most. The view – so comforting to the rich – that inequality provides a spur for economic progress which benefits the poor is no more true at the scale of a town than at the scale of the nation. Meanwhile, cities whose economies are in trouble tend also to be more unequal than most in their distribution of rewards.

This chapter offers no easy solutions for the problems of depressed cities, but it does suggest directions of development. The longer-run improvement of the troubled cities will depend on effective national and regional policies for economic development. Cities cannot solve their problems by themselves. But we must give economic development a higher priority and target it at the most vulnerable groups – particularly the long-term unemployed and the unskilled who get left behind as economic revival begins.

The worst decay and disorder afflict neighbourhoods where the powerless and the poor live. Any renewal initiative should be used as an opportunity to consult and involve them, to confer real power on their representatives, and to develop their skills, opportunities and incomes.

Leaders in the private sector have hard-nosed economic reasons for working towards these same objectives. They are stake holders in the city. Its reputation and social health and the quality of life it offers to all its citizens are profoundly important to the enterprises operating there. The quality of life, even for rich executives, depends partly on the conditions of the poor.

New initiatives can only be effectively mobilised in the community and the private sector if local government gives them sustained and consistent leadership. Local authorities responsible for the most badly stricken cities will need funds from the national taxpayer and political support from the central government. They are dealing with the tougher aspects of worldwide economic problems and cannot cope unaided. Financial support implies an obligation to make sensible use of it; but it must be given on terms which strengthen, rather than destroy, local civic leadership, and so leave the city better equipped to tackle its own problems.

QUESTIONS

1 Make a spot check on my assertion that, once new techniques have become familiar, technological progress usually reduces the skill required to do a job. Ask your oldest friends or relatives how exactly they used to do their main paid jobs or their housework during their youth. Do they think that modern ways of doing this work demand more, or less, skill and persistence?

   Then double check: ask those now doing these jobs if they would find it easier to do them with the devices your elderly friends or relatives used in the past.

2 Pick a town you know well and identify parts of it which seem to make it easy for all classes, races and age groups to mingle easily and happily, and other parts which tend to divide the town's citizens by excluding some kinds of people, or by making it difficult for strangers to meet and get to know each other.

   What are the distinctive features which have these different effects? Do they suggest that it is always the state or always market mechanisms which are the source of the trouble?

3 Indiscriminate attempts to promote employment rarely provide jobs for those who have been out of work for a long time. How would you "target" job creating initiatives to ensure that these people stand a better chance of benefiting from them?

4 You meet a private developer who says he would like to take over a run-down council estate and do it up, provided the council first rehouses all the tenants somewhere else. What would you say to him?

   The convener of the Housing Committee says he intends to knock down the houses as soon as funds are available, and rebuild the whole estate. What would you say to him?

5 How would you decide whether the town you know best is becoming a more equal or a less equal place as time goes by? What kinds of information would you need in order to keep track of such trends?

6 What should national governments be doing to make the task of those renewing stricken cities a bit easier? This is the scale of action I turn to next.

8 | The national agenda

Starting point

I began the second half of this book by looking at the smallest scales of human action. Even in times when the ideas which I am offering are out of fashion at the centres of power, there are people who are trying to put them into practice as best they can in the places where they live and work. If we believe that we have to wait until our political friends capture power before we can set about changing the world, we shall find that they will not know what to do with power when they get it and the opportunity will be lost.

Nevertheless, it is at the national scale that the most important changes must be brought about. This chapter outlines the problems which progressive movements have to tackle on that scale. It is not a manifesto – still less a detailed plan of action. It is a sort of agenda, with explanatory notes. In six brief sections I shall discuss: (1) employment, (2) policies for incomes, (3) social policies, (4) their implications for citizenship, (5) support for families with young children, and (6) the management of public services. Each deserves a book to itself. This is no more than an essay in strategic thinking.

Next I turn briefly to some of the very important issues neglected in this essay – civil liberties, race, and so on – not to provide a condensed postscript on these, but to show why we shall make better progress with them if we start with the social and economic problems on which I have chosen to concentrate. Then, following the pattern of previous chapters, I draw a bead on the enemy to clarify what I am arguing for by showing what I am arguing against.

Full employment

As Table 8.1 shows, in Britain, as in many other countries, the growth of unemployment has swelled the numbers excluded from the mainstream of society. Unemployment afflicts whole families – whole streets. Those out of work are more likely than the rest of us to have unemployed partners, children and neighbours. Meanwhile the public, opinion polls show, have less sympathy for people who are out of work than they have for other groups such as the aged and the disabled, who also depend on the state. Governments encourage those attitudes when they treat people out of work less generously and more suspiciously than others who have to live on state benefits. Unemployment also helps to drive down the wages of the less skilled workers, making it harder for trade unions to organise them and easier for employers to recruit part-timers for insecure, low paid work. These are further causes of the growth of poverty.

There are many others who feel the chill that high unemployment spreads through the economy: ethnic minorities; pensioners who find it harder than it should be to postpone retirement or to retain a part time job; lone parents who would rather go to work than live on social security payments; prisoners who should be encouraged to earn money to compensate their victims and to support their own families; people with physical or mental handicaps who are capable of work but find it impossible to get a job; delinquents and addicts whose chances of taking up a more normal life depend heavily on opportunities for work: excluded people, all of them, who are likely to suffer more than their share of poverty and pain. Anyone who writes full employment off as unimportant or unattainable is writing off all these people.

The government seems to believe that growing prosperity in the south east of England and neighbouring regions will eventually spread to all parts of the country. But as jobs and incomes grow in the south east, so do congestion and inflationary pressures of various kinds. The government then feels compelled to rein in inflation by putting up interest rates, long before the rising tide of economic revival flows into the deprived regions of the United Kingdom, or even into the more impoverished neighbourhoods of prosperous southern cities. What does not flow naturally must be moved in other ways. A convincing strategy for higher employ-

8.1 Unemployment in different countries

Standardised unemployment rates in selected OECD countries

Per cent of total labour force

	1979	1980	1981	1982	1983	1984	1985	1986	1987	1988	1989
Canada	7.4	7.4	7.5	10.9	11.8	11.2	10.4	9.5	8.8	7.7	7.5
United States	5.8	7.0	7.5	9.5	9.5	7.4	7.1	6.9	6.1	5.4	5.2
Japan	2.1	2.0	2.2	2.4	2.6	2.7	2.6	2.8	2.8	2.5	2.3
Australia	6.2	6.0	5.7	7.1	9.9	8.9	8.2	8.0	8.0	7.2	6.1
Belgium	8.2	8.8	10.8	12.6	12.1	12.1	11.3	11.2	11.0	9.9	9.0
Finland	5.9	4.6	4.8	5.3	5.4	5.2	5.0	5.3	5.0	4.5	4.4
France	5.9	6.3	7.4	8.1	8.3	9.7	10.2	10.4	10.5	10.0	9.5
Germany	3.2	3.0	4.4	6.1	8.0	7.1	7.2	6.4	6.2	6.1	5.5
Italy	7.6	7.5	7.8	8.4	8.8	9.4	9.6	10.5	10.9	11.0	10.9
Netherlands	5.4	6.0	8.5	11.4	12.0	11.8	10.6	9.9	9.6	9.5	—
Norway	2.0	1.6	2.0	2.6	3.4	3.1	2.6	2.0	2.1	3.2	4.9
Spain	8.5	11.2	13.9	15.8	17.2	20.0	21.4	21.0	20.1	19.1	16.9
Sweden	2.1	2.0	2.5	3.2	3.5	3.1	2.8	2.7	1.9	1.6	1.4
United Kingdom	5.0	6.4	9.8	11.3	12.4	11.7	11.2	11.2	10.2	8.3	6.4
Seven major countries	4.9	5.5	6.4	7.7	8.1	7.3	7.2	7.1	6.7	6.1	5.6
EEC Total	5.7	6.4	8.2	9.5	10.4	10.7	10.8	10.8	10.5	9.8	8.9
OECD Total	5.1	5.8	6.7	8.1	8.6	7.9	7.8	7.7	7.3	6.7	6.1

Source: OECD, Quarterly Labour Force Statistics, 1990, No. 1, Paris, 1990

ment will have to include policies to promote growth in the lagging regions, to transfer work there from the south, and to focus resources for job creation on particular disadvantaged neighbourhoods and groups within cities.

Incomes policies

The struggle for full employment will call for one feature which is crucially important, but evaded by both the main parties: this is a policy for incomes. The changes in economic structure discussed in the last chapter led many countries into inflation during the 1970s, while the oil price explosion caused balance of payments difficulties which could only be brought under control by reducing real incomes and living standards.

Different countries made these adjustments in different ways. Countries like Sweden, with a strong corporate and collective tradition among unions and employers, kept earnings converging towards greater equality – at least until recently. Meanwhile they brought about a steady reduction in real incomes which helped to bring international payments back into balance and to keep unemployment really low – far below the US figures. To compensate skilled workers who have foregone wage increases while their employers prospered from wage restraint, the state in Sweden levied a tax on profits to build up a fund that is invested in industry for the benefit of all workers.

Those like the United States, with weak trade union movements and little capacity for coherent collective action among employers, achieved the reduction in incomes largely through market forces which brought down wages. The human impact has been pretty brutal: the real incomes of families with children have fallen, and by 1985 the US Congressional Budget Office was reporting that they accounted for two-thirds of those in poverty – despite the fact that the numbers of households with children had also fallen. However, inflation was brought under control and unemployment, by American standards, remains low.

Britain, with fairly strong unions, but little capacity for coherent joint action among them, and still less among employers, has kept the wages of organised workers and the rich moving forward aggressively, generating high inflation. It has also allowed much larger numbers of people to fall out of work than most countries would tolerate. This "strategy" is expensive for the state, wasteful of human life and talent, and damages national unity and decent human relations. Expenditure on the police and prisons has become one of the great growth areas of government.

Why have we taken this dangerous road? It is widely believed in the main British parties that incomes policies have failed. They worked pretty well for short periods (most recently between 1975 and 1978) but then broke down, with results which scarred the memories of all concerned. That is why we now have the "incomes policy" of keeping large numbers of people out of work. In the short run it works. But meanwhile, the top tenth and the bottom half in the UK as a whole have drifted further and further apart, as Table 8.2 shows.

Table 8.3 shows how the earnings of men in full time manual jobs have changed over the longer term. For nearly a century the earnings of the poorest tenth fluctuated between 66 and 70 per cent of the median figure – the earnings of those in the middle of the income range. Then, after 1982, they began to fall further

8.2 Changes in the distribution of incomes

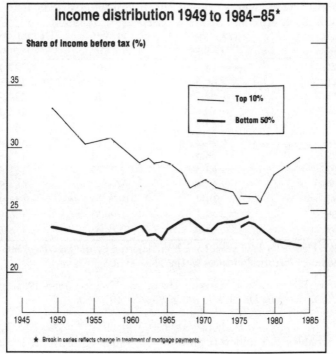

Income distribution 1949 to 1984–85*

— Share of income before tax (%)

| Top 10% |
| Bottom 50% |

35

30

25

20

1945   1950   1955   1960   1965   1970   1975   1980   1985

★ Break in series reflects change in treatment of mortgage payments.

Source: John Hills, *Changing Tax*, London, Child Poverty Action Group, 1988, p.8.

behind. Meanwhile the earnings of the richest tenth began to draw further ahead of the median.

We do not know if this trend is a temporary result of changes in industrial structure, or whether it is going to go a lot further; it is a pattern to be seen all over Western Europe. But in Britain, government has certainly exacerbated these divisive trends. As Tables 8.4 to 8.6 show, it has used the tax and benefit systems to tip the scales still further against poorer families. Table 8.4 divides the population into ten groups of "taxable units", each of equal size, ranked by the amount of their income in relation to their needs (taking account of family size and ages). Group 1 are the poorest; group 10 the richest. All in the lower half of the income distribution have suffered. The gains have been heaped on the richest.

Making our future

8.3 Long-term changes in income inequality

Dispersion of earnings of full-time men in manual jobs, 1886–1989.

Year	Lowest decile as % of median	median (£)	Highest decile as % of median
1886	68.6	1.21	143.1
1906	66.5	1.47	156.8
1938	67.7	3.40	139.9
1960	70.6	14.17	145.2
1970	67.3	25.60	147.5
1976	70.2	62.10	144.9
1979	68.3	88.20	148.5
1982	68.3	125.20	152.6
1986	65.4	163.40	154.8
1987	64.4	173.90	155.9
1988	64.3	188.00	156.5
1989	63.9	203.90	158.2

Note: Figures for later years have been adjusted by the Low Pay Unit to take account of statistical changes in the New Earnings Survey.

Source: British Labour Statistics Historical Abstract: 1886–1986, HMSO, 1971, updated by DE New Earnings Surveys 1970–89.

Tables 8.5 and 8.6 present the same patterns in a different way by showing the percentage of people in each group who gained during the decade (Table 8.5) and the percentage who lost (Table 8.6). Nearly all the richest fifth of the people gained something. Nearly all the poorest half lost.

Between 1980 and 1985, no country in the European Community achieved as large an increase in the numbers in poverty as the UK did (defining poverty as a living standard less than 50 per cent of the national average). These trends may eventually lead to serious trouble. We have not since the Second World War produced a racist demagogue to mobilise anxious workers and the unemployed, but one may be waiting in the wings. Ulster shows the way things could go.

A consensus on a broadly fair distribution of incomes and benefits would check this socially dangerous trend; but, just as important, it would help to achieve better economic management. Reduced inflationary pressures would lessen the need to restrict growth; the consequent reduction in unemployment would reduce the number of people potentially in poverty, and release resources

8.4 Gains and losses of different income gruops

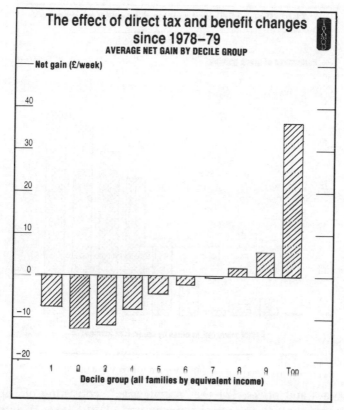

The effect of direct tax and benefit changes since 1978–79
AVERAGE NET GAIN BY DECILE GROUP

Net gain (£/week)

40

30

20

10

0

−10

−20

1 2 3 4 5 6 7 8 9 Top
Decile group (all families by equivalent income)

Source: John Hills, op. cit., p.13.

to deal with the problems that would remain. This is a true "virtuous circle", and there is no excuse for abandoning the effort to achieve it simply because we have made mistakes in the past. In a changing economy the effort will certainly have to take new forms. Trade unions have lost membership and authority. More tasks are being subcontracted to people who are self-employed, and thus outside any social contract of this kind.

Doubtless the procedures needed will not be called an "incomes policy", but the essential requirement for a consensus, as continental experience shows, is still an agreement between the government, the employers and the unions – the "social partners" as they are called in other parts of Europe – dealing with: (1) money

8.5 Who gained

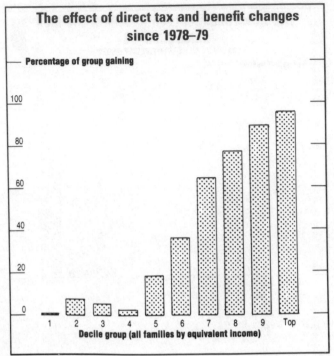

The effect of direct tax and benefit changes
since 1978–79

Percentage of group gaining

Decile group (all families by equivalent income)

Source: John Hills, op. cit., p.13.

incomes and prices; (2) the "social wage", consisting of benefits
provided through the social services; and (3) the taxes required to
finance these services. All have distributional implications which
help to shape the living standards of different groups. It is these
patterns – not just the general growth of wages – which matter
most to people. The concept of a "fair wage" goes back to
medieval times. What we need today – because it's what people
are mainly concerned about when they discuss "income justice" –
is a concept of "fair differentials".

What is a fair relationship between (say) the top and bottom
fifths of the workers within any organisation or profession? That is
the kind of question we have to address. In Britain, where people
are more prudishly secretive about income than about sex, we
have a long way to go before these matters can even be discussed,
yet a sense of common citizenship cannot develop while one of the
fundamental bases of fellowship or comradeship is shrouded in a

8.6   Who lost

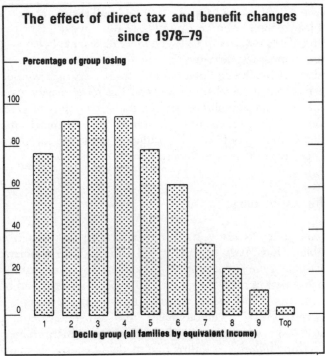

The effect of direct tax and benefit changes since 1978–79

— Percentage of group losing

Source. John Hills, op. cit , p 13

conspiracy of embarrassed silence. Try posing these questions in a newspaper article, or on a radio or television show in Britain. (I have.) Sub-editors, producers, presenters, cut you straight out of their paper or programme. Try posing them at a church seminar on "social justice", attended by ministers and elders: the chairman swiftly moves the conversation on to other issues – aware, probably, that his church has no publicly defensible basis for deciding the pay even of its own clergy. The Swedes have a much saner attitude to such things: everyone's tax return – like all official documents – is available for public inspection. Proposals for a statutory minimum wage, now being formulated in the Labour movement, may open up the debate in Britain. But this is only a beginning. A minimum wage without a maximum is an argument without a conclusion.

A consensus on distribution does not have to be rigid or formalised: Japan achieves a far more equitable distribution than

Britain or the US simply because agreements at every level are informed by a sense of mutual obligation rather than of confrontation. The economic results speak for themselves. Agreements may, as in Italy, be more or less explicitly restricted to large companies, leaving the small enterprises to market forces, and yet still achieve large benefits for society as a whole. What is clear is that if social provision and the relief of poverty are to be more than an ambulance service for the victims of greed, and if economic progress is not constantly to over-reach itself, then radicals must confront the difficult questions of distributional justice. Evasion has proved too costly.

The social wage

Social policy is not something to turn to only when economic problems have been solved. It is itself one of the problems, and at the same time an essential foundation for their solution. How much a nation needs to spend on its social services and how much people can afford to pay in taxes to support them depend heavily on the levels of employment and unemployment, and the distribution of incomes. In countries which have adopted something like the Scandinavian model of economic management, the growth and distribution of social services and of the taxes required to pay for them play important parts in the annual negotiation about investment and incomes. These costs cannot be evaded by failing to talk about them. In the US, wage negotiations are increasingly dominated by demands for health and pension benefits which the state fails to provide; this is now the main element in cost inflation. In Britain, high rates of unemployment and an increasingly unequal distribution of incomes have put a lot more people into poverty, and therefore raised expenditure on social services.

In addition, the social services in most advanced countries have to care for a growing population of the very old, and to help growing numbers of one parent families. Technological advances – particularly in health care – increase the cost of the rising standards of care which they make possible. Meanwhile, we in Britain have promised ourselves growth in the social services which will be expensive to provide – higher education for the growing proportion of qualified young people, for example, and

better pensions for those retiring in future years.
These burdens mean that progress is bound to be slow. The
era of rapid expansion in the social services is over. But we need
clear principles of social policy even more urgently when social
expenditure is static or declining than when it is growing. We will
want, whenever possible, to bring the poorest people into pension
schemes, schools, health services and other programmes which
everyone uses. That helps to eliminate stigma, and to create a
shared sense of citizenship. Furthermore, the benefits offered by
some services depend partly on the other people using them.
School pupils and college students have always learnt as much
from their fellow students as from their teachers – often more. If
we have a special concern for the less advantaged, then it is vital
that they should work in classes with a broad mix of abilities and
not be confined to a ghetto of the outcasts and outlaws.

Public services used by everyone can also create a setting in
which it is easier to maintain proper professional relationships
which are designed to serve, not to exploit, the customers. The
fashionable alternative, the market, does not do this, despite the
claims made for it. It was fitting for Margaret Thatcher to express
horror when private clinics buy organs for transplantation; but she
should not have been surprised. This is only a more than usually
flagrant example of the kind of thing that is to be expected when
medical care is handed over to the profit motive. We know where
it ultimately leads. Try getting into a New York hospital if you
have been smashed up by a mugger but have no medical insurance
– as a friend of mine did. They just called a taxi for him. Passing
laws against such abuses and recruiting a police force of inspectors
to enforce them does not tackle the wider corruption which
market morality too easily brings into public services.

The corruption is not confined to wholly private systems.
Once there is enough private practice around, consultants in the
public system have an interest in lengthening the queues which
can be jumped by people prepared to pay privately for their
services. Most doctors don't behave like that, but we are steadily
building for them an environment in which it is more tempting to
behave badly, harder to be good. It is the job of government to set
incentives in the opposite directions. This does not mean that
every public service has to be provided free, or that every customer
has to be charged the same amount for it. There are good reasons,
for example, to charge fees to those who gain the lifelong

privileges conferred by a university education, and for relating those charges to parents' incomes. Later, perhaps, all income tax payers who have gained a degree should pay a modest graduate tax as a contribution towards the education of their successors.

To provide public services at a decent standard costs a lot of money. Again the principles outlined in earlier chapters offer guidance to the best ways of raising these funds. National insurance contributions and direct taxes have major advantages over private insurance and charitable funding. They are cheaper to administer. They can easily be made progressive, so that they take more from the rich than the poor. They do not lead to exclusion of the "bad risks" – the more vulnerable people who are most likely to need expensive care. Public funding also helps to give people a sense that they have rights, when they need them, to a service for which they have paid their "subscription".

If it is politically difficult to raise more money from taxes and insurance contributions we may have to wait until public funds are freed by further reductions in unemployment and the costs of benefit for those out of work. That will take time. The reduction of tax reliefs which confer their most generous benefits on the rich – on mortgage interest, and on insurance and pension contributions for example – is another obvious and just source of revenue. Table 8.7 compares the cost – in public spending, and in tax foregone –

8.7 Some social security benefits and tax reliefs

£ millions: UK 1988–89 estimates			
Benefits			Tax Reliefs[2]
Insurance benefits[1]		Income tax allowances	
Retirement pensions	19,390	Married man's	12,900
Widows' benefits	908	Single person's	8,600
Unemployment benefit	1,143	Reliefs for pensioners	
Invalidity benefit	3,410	Employers' contributions	2,600
War pensions	603	Employees' contributions	1,700
Means-tested income support	7,814[3]	Investment income of pension	
Housing benefit	3,817	schemes	4,400
Child benefit	4,522	Pensioners' lump sums	1,000
		Interest on loans to owner	
		occupiers	5,500

Notes

[1] Basic, plus earnings related and (for pensioners) Christmas bonus

[2] Costs to the Exchequer of reliefs

[3] Including net payments of £164m. from Social Fund

Source: The Government's Expenditure Plans, 1989, Chapter 15, January 1989.

of a few of the main social security benefits and tax reliefs. Several of these reliefs transfer larger sums of money than all but the largest social security benefits. But to eliminate them will take time – you cannot suddenly wipe out cash benefits on which people have founded their whole family economy.

Family support

Running through every branch of a progressive social policy is a central priority. As Table 8.2 showed, families with dependent children make up a large and growing proportion of the people in poverty in Britain. The real value of child benefit has fallen, and the prices of the things which these families have to spend a lot of their money on – rent, fuel and food, for example – have risen faster than the rest of the cost of living. These trends deepen the first two troughs of the lifetime cycle of alternating poverty and affluence through which many people pass. Most of us suffer most severe economic stress in childhood, in early parenthood and in old age – the three phases in life when earnings sufficient to support a worker may fail adequately to meet the needs of dependent members of the household. Like every industrial country, we have recognised the third trough – though less generously than most of them – by organising ways of transferring income from those in the prime of life to those who have retired. But we have never recognised the needs of children to the same extent, although for the future health and welfare of the nation it is even more important to do so. But in Britain child benefit and its predecessors – family allowance and child tax allowance – have never made more than a small contribution to the cost of caring for a child: a lot less than income support payments for children, and far less than foster care payments. (Things are very different in some other European countries.)

To fill this deficiency, successive governments have built up an elaborate array of means-tested payments for low paid working families with children (some of which are available to the childless too). These include family credit and housing benefit, which are the two biggest, together with free school meals, free prescriptions under the health service, and many other smaller means tested benefits. These have never been popular; they do not grow naturally out of British traditions. They also work very badly; they are expensive to administer, and only about half the people entitled to these benefits actually take them up. When combined with income tax which "tapers in" at low income levels, these benefits taper out with rising income, and create nasty poverty traps. Lone parents and low paid two-parent families are apt to find that however hard they work, they cannot significantly increase their spendable incomes.

Every British politician knows that voters are hostile to any possibility that people living on social security benefits might get as high an income as those who go out to work. When benefits really do come close to wage levels, it is nearly always a family with several children that is involved. Thus the earnings of low paid workers with several children provide, in effect, a political ceiling to the benefits which any government is prepared to pay to similar families when they are out of work. The payments made to large families then determine the successively lower payments which can be made to smaller families, the childless and the single. The question, How can we raise the incomes of low paid workers with several children? is therefore a vital one for all the poorest people, whether they have children or not.

The answer should ideally start from an incomes policy which raises the incomes of the lowest paid closer to the average. After that, child benefit provides much the best way of helping these families. It is cheap to administer. It is very efficient, reaching 100 per cent of the people entitled to get it. It inflicts no poverty trap. It is paid direct to the mother, who thus has a secure and predictable flow of cash which will continue to come to her if she starts work or gets a better job. And – most important of all – it expresses an important commitment on behalf of all of us to the support of children, and the nation's future.

So, with all these advantages, why has child benefit, already inadequate, been allowed to wither away? Partly because it costs a lot. An increase of £1 over the present weekly figure of £7.25 would cost £670 millions a year which is about one-third of a penny in the pound on income tax. That problem might be resolved by transforming the married man's tax allowance into a family benefit, which would help him more generously during the years when he most needs it. (This is the most indiscriminately wasteful tax allowance, reflecting the long-dead assumptions that only the middle class paid income tax, and that middle class wives had to give up their jobs when they got married.)

150

Partly because it has never been adequate, child benefit is even less popular than benefits for the unemployed with the British electorate. The TUC's annual congresses are far more likely to demand an increase in old age pensions – or (until it was abolished) the death grant – than an increase in child benefit. There is a battle for hearts and minds still to be fought here. The strategic point is that anyone concerned about raising the incomes of poor people of any kind must start with the low paid worker with several children. That is because they have been losing ground for years; because they are responsible for the development of the children upon whose future capacities we all depend; and because their living standards determine what can be done for anyone else who is poor.

Treating people right

Stein Ringen, who has made the best review of research on the "welfare states" of the affluent democracies, concluded that the people of these countries remain solidly convinced that they need their social services. But they are quite critical about the performance of these services. Since every study of the matter tends to show that a large part of the huge increase in funds devoted to social services since the Second World War has been used to make life better for their staff rather than to improve the service delivered to the customers, the citizens have some reason to be critical.

Britain is no exception to these patterns. When the government elected in 1979 set about cutting and privatising bits of the welfare state, the people who protested marched under the banners of NALGO, NUPE, COHSE, the NUT and other public service unions. They were right to march; but their protests would have carried much greater weight if it had been the enraged pupils and their parents, the Health Service patients, the council tenants and the clients of the social workers who had turned out in protest. It scarcely ever was.

After years of Tory attrition, many on the Left feel tempted to defend every feature of the "welfare state". Progressives must not fall into this very conservative posture. They must formulate their own plans for reforming the management and practices of the social services. Monopolies of every kind are dangerous – and particularly so when their staff or their customers are powerless or poverty stricken people. Whenever possible, people should have some choice about where they go for help. The job of those who manage a social service must be to determine what people need, to know what is available in the area, to add to that if necessary, and to get the best possible deal for their customers. Defending the interests of their staff is the job of trade unions. Local managers will need budgets with delegated spending powers, and much better information than most of them have had hitherto about comparative costs and value-for-money. Services will need to be monitored to ensure that they do not fall into strata of varying quality, serving people of different incomes and classes – the weakest getting the worst.

People should be helped to organise their own services and to speak for themselves wherever possible. Such initiatives will not be taken everywhere; but all key staff should gain experience of working for community-based groups. It is surprising how often the "experts" (in mental health, in dealing with the homeless, in adult education and so on) gain a new perception of their customers' capacities when these customers become their employers. Residential institutions, in particular, should be as open as possible. People still capable of being shocked if they see things going wrong should pass through them each day: the relatives of residents, the postman, and the ordinary plumbers, doctors and priests working in the surrounding community, not people hired to work full time in such services. Many of these approaches can be tried out locally without waiting for a national programme.

I could continue, but enough has been said to show that public services can be made more "user friendly"; their staff can be given a greater sense of accountability to those whom they serve and helped to see them as ordinary human beings; and the poorest people can be included without unnecessary distinctions. Forward-looking services are already moving in these directions. Training people in the public service to work in new ways will be a slow job; but next time there has to be a demonstration against attacks upon the "welfare state" the customers may be out on the picket lines with the staff.

Other business

Civil liberties, better race relations, women's rights, gay rights and the hopes expressed by "green" politics are not less important than the issues of inequality, poverty and public service discussed here. But to seek stronger legal protection for civil liberties without first providing economic opportunities and security, and the more open, responsive public services which make it easier for the poor and the powerless to claim these rights, would only benefit the comfortable. Equally, the most potent force against discrimination against women, blacks and gays would be a return to full employment, which would also encourage more privileged groups to accept minorities without fear of competition for their own jobs.

That does not mean that we should postpone the struggle against discrimination until every other problem has been solved; but unless we make some progress towards economic equality, that struggle will only enable the abler or luckier members of the excluded groups to escape, depriving those left behind of leadership. The fate of black Americans in the ghettos today should be an example and a warning to all of us. The abler and more fortunate blacks have achieved great advances, but the majority are worse off than before. To cheer on oppressed and exploited people as they scramble for a slightly larger share of the goodies offered by an increasingly unequal society is scarcely a radical act.

The opposition

The opposition to the ideas in this chapter takes many forms, and there is space here only for the more strident voices. There are people intent on extending the sway of market mechanisms and restricting that of the state in the names of freedom and accountability to customers. If you look at some public housing estates, or at the ways in which the state-owned nuclear power industry has responded to public anxiety, you have to concede that they have a point. But in a market, you only have as much freedom and choice as you can pay for. Unless advocates of market-based freedom support calls for a more equal distribution of income, their arguments are hypocritical.

There are those who are obsessed by the problem of "incentives to work" amongst people who depend on social security payments. "Welfare junkies", they would call them, sunk in a "dependency culture". Many of us can name someone to whom these harsh words could perhaps be fairly applied. But we would take the critics' moral outrage more seriously if they supported moves to increase payments like child benefit, which free people from the poverty traps that deter them from returning to work, and ensured that there are enough jobs for all who want them.

There are those who want to shift responsibilities of many kinds (from caring for the aged to preventing delinquency among the young) onto "the family". These we could take more seriously if they were determined to increase housing benefit, and to ensure that other things like good housing and health services are available to help families bear these responsibilities. They should also be told that a great deal of research has been done on the incentive effects of benefits. Higher insurance benefits will probably increase the numbers who go to work; they offer rights worth qualifying for. Nor do people leave decent jobs to live on benefit. However, if they have been out of work for a long time they may find it difficult to resume work – especially if they depend on benefits which will be withdrawn as they start to earn. However, not even this "unemployment trap" raises the number out of work; it simply means that the long-term unemployed are less likely to fill the vacancies which arise. Others are eager to do so.

Then there are those who are determined to abolish universal services, such as child benefit, paid as of right to whole categories of people, and replace them with means tested benefits paid on a more selective basis to those in greatest need. They argue that this is a more "efficient" way of relieving poverty. But they forget the problem of "take-up", and neglect the ways in which these payments are financed. The net effect of child benefit, coupled with the income tax payments which finance it – even from our very gently progressive income tax – is to take money away from the rich (because of their higher tax rates) and from the childless (who get no benefit), and give it to poor and middle-income families with children (giving most of all to the poorest and to the largest families). That seems pretty fair and efficient.

More fundamentally, however, this argument about "targeting

the poor" displays a morally coarse understanding of what the social services are for – what they are supposed to be "efficient" at. If the aim is to build a society with a shared sense of citizenship – concerned about the welfare of all its members, and particularly concerned about the youngest and the frailest – then means tested benefits, administered in tiresome or humiliating ways, benefits which are only taken up by about half the people entitled to them, are not "efficient". But child benefit is.

Demolishing these arguments point by point is easy enough, but fails to explain why those who advance them have nevertheless won the day, electorally speaking, for many years. Services which are mainly important to the powerless and the poor – like unemployment benefit, council housing and rent restrictions – have been steadily eroded. The media rarely give these matters much attention. Powerlessness is real.

But the services which are important to the middle classes, whether as customers or as staff – like education and the National Health Service – are retained or even expanded. Although tax relief on mortgage interest has been falling in real terms for each borrower, it is still growing in total, while subsidies for public housing are being cut back; but noone calls the middle class people who benefit most from all this "welfare junkies" or "victims of a dependency culture".

People sense which way the world is moving. Many feel that for the sake of their families they must choose the private option, pay the premiums for private medical care, buy their way into a neighbourhood with nice schools – and let the Devil take the hindmost. The Labour movement, for reasons which I shall come to, makes a rather confused response to all this. Thus, borne onwards by the momentum created by their own acts, the Conservatives have repeatedly lost the intellectual and moral argument but won the elections.

Conclusion

I will try to summarise the national priorities of a progressive strategy, based on the principles outlined in the first half of this book. These are its essentials.

[1] Move back towards much higher levels of employment,

reducing the devastating waste of human capacities suffered by those now out of work, and deliberately creating scarcities of labour at the bottom end of the labour market.

[2] Develop workable incomes policies, set within an evolving consensus about industrial investment, the growth and distribution of incomes, the social wage and tax policies – demonstrating a capacity for responsible, collective citizenship which makes it possible to achieve faster economic growth and lower levels of unemployment.

[3] Develop a more efficient, responsive, democratic system of social services, which gives first priority to those with greatest needs, while enabling everyone to share in its benefits – a system which welcomes and supports independent initiatives from community-based groups.

[4] Raise the incomes of families with children who depend on low wages – "the working poor" – particularly through improved child benefits and a more equal distribution of earnings, recognising that the living standards of these families help to determine the prospects for many of the next generation, and that they fix the political ceiling for the incomes of everyone else now living in poverty.

That these things can be done is not in doubt: there are countries which have achieved most of them. Every opinion poll shows that the British have not abandoned their concerns for vulnerable people, for the social policies which could help them, or for the moral values expressed by these policies. For many years, however, there has not been an opposition party which they were prepared to trust.

The opposition may soon return to power. But the rebuilding of an effective alternative to the previous regime may take a good deal longer. It will certainly be a difficult task. Consider some of the main political priorities we have identified: (1) an incomes policy, which must for considerable periods of time hold the wages of skilled workers below the levels which an aggressive union could get for them; (2) the development of child benefit, or other benefits unrelated to wages, for families with children; and (3) an opening up, diversification and democratisation of the social services which would break up monopolies and give their customers more power. Powerful trade unions have resisted all these things in the past. Many still do.

There is no point in bashing the unions. They are us, acting collectively in our capacity as workers. Slow though they have sometimes been to respond, they have in these bad times helped to protect the less skilled, the ethnic minorities and women – those of them, that is to say, who get into the industries where unions are strong. Professional associations, trade associations and the Confederation of British Industry are often much less generous or imaginative. All these institutions represent people at work, and work accounts for no more than half our waking hours for less than half our lifetimes (averaging for men and women).

Can we, through the Labour movement, bring together a more coherent and humane concern for the whole life span and for all our needs? Unions have already gone a long way towards incorporating the needs of the retired in their thinking. "Half pay in retirement" has long been one of their slogans. But how about mothers and children, the long-term unemployed, and those whose handicaps prevent them from ever getting a job? Many of these will be relatives of union members. If unions cannot extend their concern to these people, we shall have to rely on political parties, churches and other movements which can. Trade unions would then retain an important, but limited, role as guardians of our workplace interests, but they would no longer play a central part in broader movements concerned with the whole nation's future. I come back to these questions in the final chapter of this book.

QUESTIONS

1 Identify two people you know: one in a reasonably well paid job, and the other living on income support, a retirement pension or some other social security payment from the state. Make an estimate of the annual value of the tax relief on mortgage interest and pension contributions received by the former and compare it with the social security payments received by the latter.

  Does the pattern seem fair? Does it seem an efficient way of using public funds to meet urgent needs?

2 You suffer from a painful, but not a life threatening, illness for which you are awaiting hospital treatment. You could afford to jump the queue and get treated as a private patient. What are the arguments for and against doing so? Should it make any difference if the illness is life threatening?

3   The government has strengthened parents' rights to choose schools and to get information about their performance, and has weakened the local authorities' powers to control the transfer of pupils between primary and secondary schools. As a result, two secondary schools in your neighbourhood are becoming increasingly polarised – one taking middle class children and the other taking working class children and ethnic minorities. Does it matter? If you think it does matter, what could be done about it?

4   I asserted that the longer-term prospects of social services under the present British government seem to depend on the extent to which they meet the needs of the middle class, whether as workers or as customers. Check my assertion against some examples of services you know about. And watch what happens in future. What would you expect to happen to the government-funded Legal Aid Scheme? How about the School Meals Service?

5   Why is it so much harder to gain public support amongst the British for child benefits than for pensions? Conduct your own straw poll amongst a few friends to test out your ideas about the answer to that question. You may want to ask them: If people give up having children, will there be any pensions?

6   Does the government's reliance on nuclear weapons as a central element in our defence seem likely to have any effects on its attitudes to the ordinary people of this country? Would a defence system which depended on a broadly-based citizen army, rather than on fearsome weapons controlled by a few men in deep bunkers, have any implications for policies about health, education, and the involvement of the people in discussions about foreign policy and defence?

9 A service for people

Why housing?

Housing plays a central part in our lives, being the shelter for our families, the storeroom for our belongings, the symbol of our status, the showcase for our possessions, and the lair from which we gain access to the world. Nations never finally "solve the housing problem". They can, however, transform it. In the years after the Second World War "the housing problem" meant, for many, a brutally urgent need for shelter. In many countries it still does. But in the Western world today, it can mean all kinds of things.

Housing conditions are shaped by a combination of national, regional and local agencies. All scales of action have to be considered. They depend on private, public and voluntary providers, all of whom are likely to stay in business for a long time to come.

These characteristics make housing a particularly useful field in which to try out the political principles I have outlined. I shall start by recalling these principles. Then I sketch the essential features of the field – the "policy environment" of housing. Next I focus upon action in three sections, dealing first with central government, then with local government, and thirdly with what are – rather misleadingly – called "special needs". That leads finally to the chapter's conclusions.

I shall take Britain as the setting for this discussion. But many other countries face similar problems. Indeed, my own conclusions owe a great deal to their experience.

Problems and principles

The most compelling arguments for social action start from pain.
So what kinds of pain are we talking about in the field of housing?
We are talking about the couple with two young children living in
a cold, damp caravan never intended for winter use, worrying
about where they'll go when they get turned out to make room for
the high-paying summer visitors. They're on the council's waiting
list but, as newcomers to the district, they haven't a hope of
getting rehoused. If they end up roofless, they will probably be put
into bed-and-breakfast accommodation.

We are talking about the elderly widow with her own roomy
but decaying home, with no-one to help fix the leaking roof and
no way of paying for urgently needed repairs. The council was
forced to abandon its repairs grant scheme when its spending was
"capped" by the government.

Then there's the young woman who was placed, with her
baby, in a desolate council estate when she sought refuge from a
violent husband – and is now terrorised by the equally violent
thieves and drug pushers who rule the neighbourhood. She shuts
herself in all day in the bare flat which she cannot furnish because
the Social Fund's drastically reduced "single payments" no longer
run to that.

The needs of these people are the stuff of which television
programmes are made. But there are less obvious cases of pain that
can be equally harrowing. Take the elderly man, once aggressively
fit but now confined to a wheel-chair, who has not been out for
the past two years because he cannot get down the stairs. The
council had to sell to its tenants most of the street-level houses,
one of which he had hoped to transfer to.

Or take the young couple who bought a house in London
because it was the only way they could get a home, and they
thought that by postponing having a family they could just manage
mortgage payments totalling half their joint incomes. Then
interest rates rose still higher and they found they could cope no
longer. They have put their house on the market at a price a good
deal less than they paid for it, but no-one even comes to look at it.

Or take the middle aged man who sits all day in his overcoat
in an unheated flat, knowing and seeing no-one because he has
spent the last thirty years in a hospital for the mentally
handicapped. Social workers rarely visit this neighborhood: they

160

A service for people

have more urgent cases to attend to elsewhere.

Or take the unemployed man who had to leave his family in a perfectly good house in Tyneside in order to take a job in the south where he hasn't a hope of finding a home he can afford – and now he must either go home to the dole and watch the mould gather in the rooms he can no longer heat, or stay down south in lodgings while his marriage breaks up. Meanwhile the regional policies which used to bring some jobs to Tyneside, and the housing policies which built new towns for people moving to the south have both been abolished.

Things don't go as badly as this everywhere. But these cases are real and I could add many more. They will serve to show what we are talking about. Housing problems form an interlocking pattern of pain, poverty, powerlessness and stigma which box people in – sometimes literally imprisoning them in bleak and dreary homes. Hopelessness is their common experience. Their poverty could be relieved or prevented if they were not powerless: so powerless, indeed, that the government can with impunity abolish the very programmes which used to help them. Their pain, their poverty and their powerlessness are reinforced by public neglect.

Note the diversity of these people and their problems. The mass of working class families, huddled many years ago in the smokey terraces that belonged to private landlords, were eventually able to mobilise nationwide movements for better housing. But the poor today seldom come into contact with each other. Many of them are unable to work and therefore do not belong to trade unions or any other movement which could speak for them. The policies required to help them are equally diverse – and impossible, therefore, to summarise in simple slogans.

To tackle these problems successfully we must give their victims more freedom to make choices, more freedom from anxiety, a more confident conviction that they are citizens with rights, supported by a greater sense of fellowship within a more equal society. These rights cannot simply be decreed by law: more positive action will be needed. The rights conferred by a Homeless Persons Act will not mean much if public authorities have no houses in which to shelter the homeless.

Yet we have reasons for hope. Although Britain is slipping back now, its housing conditions were greatly improved and equalised during the generation after the Second World War.

161

Similar achievements can be seen throughout Europe – largely thanks to collective action in which the state played a central part. We can resume that progress towards better things if we choose.

How can we set about doing that? First we need a clearer understanding of the world we have to deal with.

The policy environment

Whatever government we have, there are some features of the world in which the makers of housing policy have to operate that can be forecast with confidence.

The incomes of people in secure, full-time jobs have risen and are likely to go on rising, although probably not so rapidly as in recent years. Many of them have two earners in their households. But, as we have seen in previous chapters, large groups of people have been excluded from this growth in prosperity. After 1992, when the single European market is to be created, the pace of economic change will become faster still.

We know that a rising tide does not lift all boats. Indeed, in the housing field one of the first effects of a rising economic tide is an increase in house prices which benefits the more affluent people who already own houses in the richer parts of the country, and damages poorer and younger people and the less prosperous regions.

Nevertheless, more and more people are buying houses. For most of them that's the only way of getting a decent home. Whereas surveys of the British used to show that more of them wanted to buy than ever expected to do so, the latest surveys show that marginally more expect to buy than want to do so.

Two things follow directly from these trends. The growing population of poorer households – the lone parents, the older pensioners, the youngsters living on their own and the unemployed, whose total numbers are unlikely to decline – means that there will always be a lot of people who have no hope of buying a house. So the right to rent a decent home at a price which they can afford must be a central commitment of governments.

Both groups – the tenants and the buyers – will need subsidies of some sort if they are to be properly housed. Many of the tenants will need help for long periods. The buyers will usually need help only for a few years – particularly when they are starting out; sometimes if they become widowed or separated from the main earner in their families; and for some, finally, when they and their houses grow old.

We conceal these realities by a self-serving trick of the dominant classes' language which describes the now dwindling support provided for tenants as "subsidies", while the payments made to home buyers are called "tax reliefs". It would be more sensible to think of both groups as tenants (half the buyers' homes belong to a building society or some other lender who, in effect, rents them to the householders) and to recognise that both are heavily subsidised in different ways. That would remind us that we should try equally hard to make *all* these payments as fair and as efficient for their purposes as possible. At the moment we "target" what are conventionally called "subsidies" towards the poorest while dishing out tax reliefs to anyone who can borrow money on a house for any purpose – to buy a new car or a time-share in Spain perhaps.

How the large quantity of decent rented housing we shall need should be provided is an open question which I shall discuss later. But some of the basic principles of the answer to that question are clear. Monopolies of all kinds are dangerous, and particularly dangerous when the people who depend upon them are vulnerable and powerless. Competing alternatives will be needed. Meanwhile things should be organised so as to ensure that the people who manage the houses are accountable first and foremost to their customers – the tenants.

The recent collapse of house sales in many parts of southern England has recreated privately rented housing in a temporary form, as those attempting to sell have resorted to short-term letting – sometimes in disgraceful conditions of crowding and insecurity. But it is pretty clear that private landlords will not re-enter the mass market to provide good rented housing for working families on a long-term basis. Anyone from whom they could make an unsubsidised profit does better to buy their own subsidised home. Private landlords will always retain a foothold in the market, but only in specialist corners, serving people who are not housed by other providers – foreign visitors, students and people expecting to move out and buy a house soon.

Before getting too deeply immersed in the technicalities of

housing itself, we should recall that, in a world where the great majority of people have decent homes, the buildings are no longer the crucial issue. The examples of hardship which I gave at the start of this chapter show that for many people it is the place in which the house stands that now matters most. That determines whether the house provides a safe, clean, attractive setting for family life and gives all members of the household opportunities for work, education, shopping, recreation and the other things they need – or whether, on the contrary, it excludes them from most of these opportunities. The value of exactly similar houses ranges from the astronomical to the unsaleable and unlettable, depending on their location.

So, in a country at Britain's stage of development, "urban" policy is even more important than housing policy. If we create towns and neighbourhoods in which no-one with any choice in the matter would live, we shall find that, no matter how good the buildings are, the poor, the powerless and the stigmatised tend reluctantly to congregate there. They will then be neglected by investors and power holders in the public and private sectors alike, and we shall end up with problems. Civic leadership, capable of creating and defending places which everyone can be proud of is an essential foundation for housing policies.

These policies, therefore, will have to take account of the changing character of the population to be housed; the location of jobs and services; the growth and distribution of incomes; taxation and subsidies; strategies for regional and urban development; and many other things besides the building, repair and management of houses.

Central responsibilities

My aim in the rest of this chapter is not to formulate a fully fledged housing policy but to show the essential features of a policy informed by the ideas in this book – starting with the central government's responsibilities.

A healthy rate of economic development, leading us back towards full employment, urban and regional policies which work through local civic leadership to focus resources on regions and cities contending with the worst economic troubles – these are an essential foundation for a successful housing policy. Jobs are not all we need: many people in the most impoverished places cannot work. For them, pensions, unemployment, sickness and disability benefits, income support and child benefits will be more important. A generous housing benefit scheme will be needed to ensure that people can pay for adequate housing. How generous that has to be will depend on the basic levels of income provided by wages and other social benefits.

In the housing field itself the central government's key roles are to create a supportive system of taxation and subsidies and to lead and co-ordinate the nation's efforts to improve its housing. Tax reliefs for house buyers should not be abolished: they should be focussed on those who most need this help – the first-time buyers (for a few years only) and poorer people buying, modernising or repairing cheaper houses. (The Japanese have used tax reliefs in this kind of way.) The poll tax, if it survives, should be related to incomes, becoming more like a local income tax, of the sort that many other countries have. Private developers and builders are entitled to make their profits – but by building what a democratic government wants, in the places and for the people whose needs are judged to be greatest, not by underpaying lump labour and bullying planning authorities to change their policies for land use.

Among local authorities, those responsible for the more prosperous and stable places, with no need for large building and modernisation programmes, should be prepared to contribute from the surpluses they make on their housing revenue and capital accounts to funds which go back into housing in other places. Laggard authorities should be pressed to improve the worst houses, to prevent abuses and harassment, to keep their own houses in decent repair, to charge rents high enough to make that possible, and to fulfil their duties to the homeless.

This is contentious work. To gain the credibility with local civic leaders which enables them to keep things moving forward in these ways, Housing Ministers must convincingly place themselves at the head of a nationwide movement for better housing. Whatever their party, that used to be generally recognised as their main job. But Britain's Conservative government abandoned all that. For years it had a tenure policy, designed to boost owner occupation at the expense of renting, and a taxation policy, designed to reduce income tax by cutting public expenditure. Public housing was the main victim of both. Those responsible for

165

it no longer had an official spokesman in Parliament. Now an even more determined attempt is being made to break up the public sector and to reduce local authorities' powers in all fields. Meanwhile the rent paying capacity of many of the poorest people has been reduced by the introduction of a poll tax, by the imposition of new rent and poll tax burdens on people living on social assistance payments, and by the withdrawal of grants which used to help the homeless to acquire basic furniture when they were rehoused. Not surprisingly, rent arrears, the numbers on the waiting lists for housing and the numbers of young homeless people – the main victims of assistance cuts – are all rising. Meanwhile in the private sector, where more and more people have felt compelled to buy, there are signs of stress too: mortgage arrears, repossessions and exploitative, short-term tenancies are all rising. What should local authorities do about all this?

The local housing service

We shall before long have a central government that is committed to doing something more effective about the nation's housing. It was ever thus. The recurring attempts made over the years by Conservative administrations to give up having a housing policy never succeed. Last time it was the Rachman scandals which triggered the change. This time it seems likely to be the sight of people sleeping in cardboard boxes. The tragedy is that so many innocent folk have to suffer before the point is proved yet again.

It does not follow, however, that things will simply go back to what used to be regarded as normal. The state could intervene in all sorts of different ways – not necessarily through local government. It could operate through voluntary housing associations or central agencies like Scottish Homes and the Northern Ireland Housing Executive, for example.

The first task of those who lead the local housing service is to know their own towns and districts and keep track of what's going on there: what kind of people are moving in or out and why, what kinds of houses are going up, coming down, or being used in new ways – everything which throws light on the constantly changing local housing market. For that they will need systematic information gathered by their officials who should seek help from local solicitors, building societies, estate agents and developers in assembling it. But there can be no substitute for tramping the streets, knocking on doors and talking with the people. Councillors, if they do their job properly, will usually know more than anyone else about their wards.

The housing committee, through its director and senior staff, should develop a local housing strategy which responds to the most urgent local needs. Those needs may be for decent rented housing for families, or for small, easily managed units for old people, or for "starter homes" for young couples who want to gain a first foothold on the owner-occupation ladder − and often for some combination of these.

The council should then encourage investment by private developers and voluntary agencies which meets the more urgent needs − finding and preparing sites and ensuring there is a choice of house types and tenures in the right places to support opportunities developing elsewhere in the local economy.

Chapter 7 explained that every place should offer people mutually sustaining "ladders of opportunity" in different sectors of its economy, so that youngsters who do well in school are not compelled to leave town for lack of a suitable job, and people who do well in their jobs are not compelled to leave in search of a suitable house. That may mean selling council houses in neighbourhoods where there are masses of them and too few available to buy. It may also mean buying houses so that they can be let by the council in areas where there are few good rented homes. It is up to the housing strategists to keep their sector of the local economy humanely in tune with other sectors, meeting changing demands before they become urgent, "special needs". They should clear their minds of ideological preferences for (or against) rented (or owner-occupied) housing, for (or against) council ownership. Their job is to ensure, so far as possible, that people can get the kind of housing they want, buying it if they wish − but only when they are ready to do so.

Owner occupiers living on reduced incomes may need help in repairing and improving their homes − or just in hanging onto them. The housing service which arranged for many of them to buy these homes must not turn its back on them if they get into difficulties.

There must be sufficient rented housing for people who cannot buy or do not wish to. That housing is likely to be better managed if it is provided by competing suppliers, each doing their best to win their tenants' loyalty. Some, at least, of this housing should be co-operatively owned by the residents, and some of that belonging to other owners should be managed co-operatively by tenants for themselves – on the lines explained in chapter 6. All rented housing should be managed from offices readily accessible to the customers by people who feel accountable to them – not by officials shut away in town halls.

A traditional housing department which is encouraging developments of this kind will wish to avoid two dangers. If it hands over its houses to housing associations and co-operatives, it may find itself unable to meet its obligations to the homeless and other vulnerable people. Social rented housing may be "balkanised" into many uncoordinated, competing units, among which "ghettos" emerge in the dwindling public sector to which the poor and the powerless are consigned.

The local authority must therefore make contracts with each landlord (various possibilities are available) which ensure that they all play their part in meeting needs, while the public housing service monitors their performance and keeps them up to the mark. How much housing, at the end of the day, the local authority retains for itself will depend on local needs, resources and preferences. The council is unlikely to be fully effective in gaining the co-operation of other providers and supporting their initiatives unless it has a considerable stock of its own houses. But municipal housing is not the only instrument for meeting needs. In most of Western Europe the local authorities rely mainly – in Western Germany entirely – on other bodies to build and manage subsidised, rented housing.

The customers' needs are not confined to housing. They may want to get the park tidied up, the refuse cleared, or the vandals chased away by the police. They may want advice about their welfare rights – not only to housing benefit but also to pensions, free school meals and bus passes. They may want a home help for their aged mother or a social worker for their errant son. They may also want to provide services of their own, not offered by any official agency – a women's centre, a creche, workshops for new businesses to get started in. It will often be useful to bring the local offices of these services under the same roof. That can provide a more responsive and efficient organisation, and save a lot of telephoning and tramping about in the rain.

In the real disaster areas, where people and their houses have been left to rot, special initiatives will be needed, under the control of local communities. We are not short of brave examples of such initiatives. The government's plan for Housing Action Trusts, which seems mainly designed to dismember public housing and transfer it to other owners, was a crude response to these problems – so provocative that it has roused against it even the worst treated tenants in the most neglected housing estates.

These areas need responsible, healing civic leadership that develops a programme in which housing plays a central part. That programme must extend well beyond housing. It should give people confidence and training, improve services, create jobs and rebuild communities. Every investment in improving these estates should be used as an opportunity to develop local skills and generate local enterprises that will help deprived communities fight their way back into their cities' economies. In Manchester's Hulme estate the tenants are trying to develop an initiative of this kind.

The private sector too must play its part in renewing these neighbourhoods. Every firm – every university and hospital too – has a stake in the reputation of the city in which it operates. In Belfast they call it "reconciliation" – between neighbouring communities and between rich and poor, the powerful and the powerless. London, Manchester, Glasgow – every big city – have as urgent needs for reconciliation.

"Special" needs

Thus far I have dealt mainly with neighbourhoods and communities – large groups and large areas. But some of the most extreme housing needs, such as those described at the start of this chapter, afflict scattered, isolated people, not visibly concentrated in particular places: the needs of the black minorities, for example, or those of battered wives, the physically handicapped, travelling people and the single homeless. These are sometimes called "special needs" in the jargon of the housing trade. But that is a misleading phrase, suggesting that there is something abnormal about them, calling for a special response at the point where problems demand attention. Such responses then tend to build into our arrangements procedures which perpetuate the problem and reinforce the victimisation of the people concerned.

Take the example of the "single homeless" discussed in chapter 1. To describe them as having "special needs" leads, too often, to the erection of hostels built specially for them by people who never took the trouble to discover that most of the homeless hate hostels and prefer to live in ordinary houses. If we start, instead, by recognising that any of us could become homeless and then consult them about their needs, that may help to ensure that more rented housing is made available for single people, that they get enough "points" in the allocation procedures to qualify for it, that they are offered help – if they need it – in acquiring some furniture, and that advice about shopping, cooking and house-keeping will be offered to those who want it. Most of them then manage pretty well in mainstream housing and cease to be regarded as "special". The few who do need further, special help from social workers or medical staff will not benefit from it unless they first get a secure home and all the social security payments which they are entitled to.

Likewise to describe people with physical handicaps as having "special" needs encourages landlords to instal rather expensive modifications to their homes. Many of these would not have been necessary if architects had been reminded that all of us who live to our full span are likely to become at least partly disabled. Thus every house is likely to accommodate a disabled person at some point in its life and should be designed to make life easy for them.

Every supposedly "special" need demands careful thought leading to a different strategy. But these strategies have common features: a determination to consult the people who experience the need and to listen to what they have to say; a willingness to go back to the beginning and redesign systems and procedures to meet demands before they emerge as "special"; a capacity to draw in resources from other services, instead of seeking solutions only within the armoury of housing powers; and a capacity to monitor what happens, so as to reveal patterns of discrimination and hardship and put them right without compelling people to create an uproar and acquire a special label of some kind before anyone will listen to them.

These strategies also depend for their success on a large stock of rented housing in the hands of a local authority or some other publicly accountable collective owner. Left to itself, private enterprise cannot tackle these problems. Nevertheless, if private rented housing can be kept in business, it provides a vital resource, meeting *demands* without compelling people to transform them into officially recognised needs, as the public sector does.

Conclusion

To what general conclusions do these arguments lead? They should reinforce our respect for civic leadership and the capacity of good local government to create cities and neighbourhoods which people can be proud of. They also call upon us to give rights and a voice that will be heard to people who otherwise get imprisoned in appalling situations. They are a practical, collective interpretation of ancient cries for liberty, fraternity and equality. They are also a call for new forms of government which will be less hierarchical, less tied to the concerns of a particular service or profession, focusing instead upon issues and problems, in a community-based and economically oriented fashion.

To bring those things about will call for consistent policies and sustained public expenditure in areas where needs related to housing are most severe. Building and renewing bricks and mortar are tasks which can be completed relatively quickly. But building and renewing communities and local economies takes much longer. It will not be achieved unless local authorities play a central, co ordinating and enabling role in the development of housing of all kinds. How much of that housing they will have to own will depend on local needs, and the quality of the collaboration built up with other owners. The few authorities with major building programmes ahead of them will need funds from central government: others should be self supporting, with the help of housing benefits and a reformed system of tax reliefs which supports house buyers when they most need it. If local councils prove themselves capable, central funds for investment in new building and modernisation should normally pass through their hands. "Quangos" like the Housing and Development Corporations – creatures of central government, unaccountable to local people – should only operate in areas with special problems. In "social rented housing" of all kinds, tenants should be helped to take over collective management, or even ownership, of their homes if they wish to do so. Where they decline to do that, other means must be found for making local housing management accountable to them. To create such a regime we must struggle to free ourselves from the knee-jerk responses inculcated by the cruder spokesmen of the Right and Left alike: the unquestioning, ideological commitment to tenancy (or owner occupation), to public enterprise (or privatisation). The decay of once-humane, Left wing ideals into a mere imperialism of the public sector alienated those whom socialists originally set out to serve. That opened the way for a counter attack by imperialists of the private sector upon an edifice which had fewer and fewer defenders. It is not institutions but communities and people – and particularly the most vulnerable of them – who should be our main concern.

QUESTIONS

1 A new government comes to power and gives local authorities responsibility for deciding whether their tenants should have a right to buy their houses. What advice would you give about this to: (a) a central London Borough with a long waiting list which owns one-third of the houses within its boundaries; (b) a remote rural district with very few council houses; and (c) a new town in which two-thirds of the houses belong to the council?

2 What would your ideal local housing office look like, and how would its services be organised? Whom would you consult before making final decisions about this?

3 You have several million pounds to spend during the next few years on improving an appallingly decayed, inner-city council estate where 50 per cent of the people are out of work. In what ways could this money be used to improve their job opportunities and earnings?

4 You are the chairman of a housing association offering, along with others, to take over most of the council houses in your town. What proposals would you make to ensure that vulnerable people are protected and anyone who becomes homeless gets decently housed?

5 You meet someone who protests that tax relief on mortgage interest should not be regarded as a subsidy. "After all," he says, "it's my own money. The government is giving back to me." What would you say to him?

6 Governments have tried to crystallise the essentials of their housing policies in brief slogans: "homes for heros" in the 1920s, "the slum clearance campaign" in the 1930s, "fair rents" in the 1960s, "the right to buy" in the 1980s. How would you summarise in a few words the essentials of the policies Britain now needs?

10 ‖ Conclusions

Introduction

The present difficulties of progressives do not arise from the power of a reactionary philosophy but from the lack of convincing alternatives to it, and the deep and genuine divisions on the Left which flow from that confusion. This chapter summarises my attempt to address that problem. I sketch out alternative moral principles and the main political priorities to which they lead. In conclusion, I consider some of the implications of these ideas for the politics of my own country.

Making our own morality

We are all born debtors to our forbears. For those of us who live in the industrialised parts of the world, life is for most people far better than it once was – precarious or dreary though it may still be for many. The most important gifts bequeathed to us are moral values made feasible by collective action: not only the winning of individual fields from the wild, but the capacity to collaborate with neighbours over an area large enough to drain the marshes, keep the sea at bay and confine torrents within their banks; not only the development of individual productive skills, but the development of convictions about human rights and the creation of schools, capable of passing these skills on to later generations.

What can we add to these achievements for our grandchildren? Can we even hand on to them the more important things which were bequeathed to us? It is a morality and the economic and social structure which sustain it that we are slowly building. Individuals try to live up to the morality they were born

173

into. They want to be "good". But for human beings collectively, what "good" means, and how easy it is to be "good", depend on the society which they make and remake for themselves as they go along. Our political actions are inspired by a moral culture, largely inherited from those who went before us. Those actions, in their turn, help to shape the moral culture we hand on to those who come after us.

The more important occasions on which people propose new public policies are not like the invention of a better machine to achieve preordained purposes in a world which remains, in other ways, unchanged. They are more like the emergence of a new school of art or drama which educates people to see the world differently, to feel new things about it and to respond to each other in new ways. We cannot prove that one pattern is in some ultimate, universal sense, better than all the others. To explain which we prefer and why we prefer it is to explain the kind of world we would prefer to live in, the kinds of citizens we would like to have sharing it with us and the relationships we would expect them to have with each other.

We are all familiar with this process in less portentous matters. Judgments of human behaviour cannot be made in a vacuum; they have to be rooted in a practice – a set of activities undertaken by particular kinds of people and pursued for particular purposes (as parents, plumbers, anglers, artists, and so on).

We are aware, too, that practices, the institutions which sustain them, and the morality they create can be changed. Take the development of motor transport as an example. Without prior planning, it created a new practice – a new thing to be good at: the driving of motor cars. Two generations later we are struggling to incorporate into that practice new conventions about refraining from alcohol, wearing seat belts and keeping to speed limits, all of which are slowly becoming part of its morality. On a broader scale, technological, social and political changes have transformed what it means to be a good worker, a good parent, a good neighbour. These practices impinge upon each other. Changes in workplace codes bring about changes in family codes, and vice versa. But there is no authoritative, over-arching, universal code which furnishes the rules to be applied all across the board by parents, plumbers, anglers, artists and everyone else.

It will sometimes be helpful to generalise at an over-arching level about the broader principles which seem to be influential in a whole society and about the directions in which they are moving. That may lead us to talk about the expansion of human rights, new concepts of citizenship and the like: big words. But, more often than not, we shall be generalising "upwards", from our knowledge of the evolving practices of parents, plumbers and many others. If we try only to generalise "downwards", seeking authoritative guidance from universal systems of thought offered us by philosophy, religion or political ideology, we shall be placing ourselves and many vulnerable people at the mercy of the party bosses and the ayatollahs – the various high priests who interpret these faiths.

One of the purposes of the arrangements we describe as the "welfare state" is to bring about changes in human relations and the moral standards which they express and sustain. The British national dock labour scheme was introduced to give security and dignity to casual workers who used to fight each other on the quays for a few hours' work. A free health service was sought by doctors who wanted to be able to make decisions about the treatment of their patients which would be guided by human need and medical knowledge, not by the profit to be made from them. I quoted in an earlier chapter the parents, then contending with Edinburgh's elaborate pecking order of schools, who wanted good comprehensive education so that they would no longer be compelled to choose between being good parents and good citizens. Along with other more selfish motives, all these people sought to create better standards of behaviour which would be easier to live up to. That is why people are now so angered by what they see as attacks upon all these things: it is a morality that is being insulted and threatened.

A strong culture with widely shared standards of behaviour develops myths which express its morality. A myth is a story or a group of stories which help us to interpret the world we live in and to choose sides within it by offering us a drama and its cast: exploiters and victims; tricksters and straight men; heroes, heroines and villains. They originate from real people and events, and are then interpreted in ways which teach us how to behave.

The myths of a previous generation of progressives encouraged them to believe that monopolies, landlords and capitalists (all assumed to be in the private sector) were among the principal villains of the public realm, while trade unionists, labour leaders and workers in the social services were among the heroes and

175

heroines. But in a world where social services (created by labour leaders and often controlled by trade unions) have become powerful monopolies and landlords, the old trumpets blow with an uncertain note and it is no longer clear who the heroes and the villains are, or to whose gunfire progressives should march.

False prophets

There are those on the far Left who would reject this analysis because they see political decisions as the outcome of power struggles in which talk of a public morality only serves to camouflage and legitimise the self-interest of the dominant classes. There is some truth in every persistent and widely held view. This one has at least two major strengths. It rejects the assumption of many old-fashioned conservatives that their own morality is God-given and permanent, not man-made and changeable. And it recognises that powerful people do not willingly relinquish power; it has to be taken from them, and that involves conflict of some sort.

However, these assertions do not take us very far. While major changes of policy direction have to wait on events which discredit the previous regime, there is scope meanwhile for smaller changes of a less cataclysmic kind in which rational analysis and moral argument often play some part. And when the time for bigger changes comes, the use which the new power holders make of their opportunities depends on the ideas already in circulation about better ways of running the world – ideas which have often been hammered out over many years. Revolutions do not eliminate the need for moral thought and practical inquiry. Indeed, they depend on both to achieve anything worth having.

Meanwhile on the Right there are people – sometimes called neo-liberals – who take what for practical purposes amounts to a similar stand, but for different reasons. They, too, reject political analysis that is based on moral standards because they claim to believe that these are a matter for individual choice in which governments and the community at large have neither the competence nor the right to interfere. Old fashioned economics – old fashioned but still widely used – relies on similar assumptions, treating the consumer's current preferences and tastes as the unquestioned basis for all valuations.

This school of thought also has important strengths. Its emphasis on accountability to the customer is healthy. Indeed, it would be radical if it were coupled with an insistence that the customers should have equal spending power, giving them all an equal voice in what would become a much more democratic marketplace. But it rests on a view of the world which is pretty academic (in the unattractive sense of being out of touch with reality).

From the start of her premiership, Mrs Thatcher – despite her assertion that "there is no such thing as society" – knew very well that she was in the business of shaping society in ways that would influence people's values and behaviour. Governments play an important part in the making of moralities. Indeed, her remark was an example of the way in which that can be done.

When a government brings about a deterioration in public services and offers subsidies to those using a more exclusive, private version of the same services it is giving people clear signals about what the "good" spouse and parent should try to do for their own families, and what "good" sons and daughters should try to do for their aged parents. When it encourages senior managers to award themselves annual increases in pay of 25 per cent and more, while awarding its own staff – transport workers, teachers, hospital workers – increases which are sometimes less than the rise in the cost of living, it is signalling how people of different kinds are to be valued. When it puts more officials onto the job of catching unemployed people claiming benefits they should not have and sends more of them to prison, but cuts down the numbers pursuing people who evade taxes and customs duties and rarely prosecutes those who are discovered, it is giving clear messages about which is the more serious crime.

Other major institutions play their parts in these morality making processes. Building societies, banks, trade unions, local authorities, universities all have at times discriminated against women, black people, people from unpopular neighbourhoods or religions, people with disabilities of various kinds, and working class people in general. Many still do. In doing so they are expressing and perpetuating valuations of the people concerned. And when they change their policies – as many have honestly tried to do – they also exert an influence on other people's values. If we want to change our world and its moral culture we do not have to wait on governments to give a lead. On the contrary, if enough people know where they want to go, democratic governments have to follow them if they wish to retain power.

Whether on the Left or the Right, people who reject the need for hard thinking about the kind of community we should try to create are wrong – literally, mistaken about the facts. All societies have complex patterns of shared values derived from their material and cultural characteristics which their people are collectively capable of changing. And their governments play important parts in shaping those changes.

Towards a pattern of principles

If a society's moral standards are important and its most important institutions and social arrangements are those which help to shape those standards, what should be the guiding principles of our own society? And what are their most urgent political implications? Can we formulate a political tradition and political programmes to live by? What myths would symbolise these values?

Security, freedom from avoidable suffering and the fear of it – these are the most basic things people seek from society. The Jewish greeting, "Shalom!", which means rather more than "peace", says it. Trust, comradeship, hope for the future are all essential parts of it. *In Place of Fear*, the title of Aneurin Bevan's book, sums it up.

People are likely to agree on that. But they may disagree about who is to be included in the "society" whose security they are prepared to work for. They would include their immediate family and closest friends; their profession, their class, their town, their country perhaps. But Europe? the whole world? When it comes to making real sacrifices for others, most of us find that our sense of comradeship or shared citizenship flags quite early in this progression.

There is no logical compulsion, no divine authority, compelling people to go the whole way down this road. If most people can at least aspire to go as far as the borders of their own country, that defines a public realm that is worth talking about – a starting point for discussion, and a hope that we may later be able to extend its scope further. As people shed fear, and gain trust in those whom they see as their fellow citizens, they find it easier to look to the wider world beyond; but those gains can be lost. If we lived in Beirut, most of us would find it difficult to be much concerned for anyone beyond our families and our closest friends. The argument thus far focuses attention on pain – avoidable and curable suffering and the fear of it. These are the things which people wish to relieve or prevent among those whom they regard as their fellow citizens. This gives us the first element in the system of thought I am explaining. If we are to discuss collective action by the state and other large institutions – action which may affect millions of people – it will be difficult in our present world to justify strategies which do not seem likely to prevent or relieve pain in some way.

In a country like Britain today, the drive to create a good society has to be founded on five related elements. For brevity's sake, I put no numbers on the assertions which follow – give no evidence in support of them. But all of them are testable statements; much of the evidence required for this purpose is available, and some of it appears in previous chapters.

[1] *Pain*. The argument starts from preventable or remediable suffering – physical or mental – which afflicts large groups of people who bear far more than their fair share of it. We should be particularly concerned when pain of one sort (curable illness, for example) tends to be combined with pains of other kinds (bad housing, humiliation in school, dangerous working conditions, incarceration in prison or mental hospital, and so on), and when such hardships tend to be transmitted from one generation to the next.

[2] *Poverty*. Pain defined in this way tends to be concentrated amongst poor people. By poverty I mean exclusion from the evolving opportunities, living standards and life chances of the average working family. "Exclusion" is a useful word, but it sounds too hygienic. In Britain, we are talking about people living on a dreary diet, in cold, damp houses; people being treated in humiliating ways by officials, landlords and teachers; people who are often anxious about debts, the insecurity of their jobs and incomes, and uncomprehended sickness. As these sentences show, we cannot even describe poverty without talking about pain. They go together.

Some people who follow the argument this far would nevertheless add that the best way of preventing and relieving poverty and pain is to promote economic growth, because "a rising

179

tide lifts all boats". They may even add that the best way of bringing about growth is to give a lot of rich people the incentive to do so by making them even richer.

Anyone who has seen how modern economies actually run will know that this is nonsense. As soon as the tide of prosperity starts rising strongly, the Government checks it, long before it flows into the poorest neighbourhoods.

There are also more fundamental reasons for scepticism about this complacent expectation. Profoundly unequal societies constantly recreate poverty in new forms – poverty not just in the sense of failing to keep up with the Joneses, but poverty that really hurts. They do that by transforming some of the luxuries of the previous generation into necessities of the next generation. I have shown that there are places in the towns and rural areas of countries like Britain where it is increasingly difficult to live without central heating, a refrigerator and the use of a car or taxis. That's fine if you can afford better heating, a fridge and a car – new necessities which were all luxuries not long ago. But social security payments and the lower wage rates do not permit that: which may be one of the reasons why the poor get sick more often and die sooner than the rich – worrying and underfeeding themselves in order to pay their fuel bills, keep their cars on the road, and keep up the payments on the fridge.

Poverty *can* be eliminated in rich societies; but that depends more on the *distribution* of their incomes than on their level or the rate at which they grow.

[3] *Powerlessness*. The poor are not selected at random. They tend to be the people whom the powerful, in the public and the private sectors alike, can afford to neglect. They are the people whom it is not worth training; the people for whom it is not worth opening a decent shop, or a new branch of a bank or building society; the people to whom noone responds if they complain that their bins are not emptied or their vandalised call boxes are not repaired.

[4] *Stigma*. Linked to all three of these factors, and reinforcing each of them, is low public esteem; or stigma for short. The status, the appearance, the accent, the manners and self-confidence of the poor and powerless encourage neglect, contempt and hostility – not only for them but also for the neighbourhoods they live in and the services they use. Worst of all, they come to undervalue themselves and to underestimate their own capacities: which leads

180

us to the fifth element in the pattern.

[5] *Culture.* The most important thing which the dominant groups in every society own is not their wealth, but the culture – its ideas, assumptions and language. You can scarcely begin discussing a society's problems without using the words offered for this purpose by these groups: victim-blaming words which convey the dominant perceptions and obliterate the voices of the people who suffer the problems. People used to talk with condescension about "the culture of poverty" in which the poor supposedly confined themselves. In fact, it is the "culture of the prosperous" which is the main source of that exclusion.

Excluded and oppressed groups are capable of challenging and changing the dominant culture, but they can only do that by acting collectively. It is a contentious and difficult task. I shall say more in the next chapter about the circumstances which help to make it possible.

The sequence of the links in this analysis depends on the purpose for which you use it. Arguments for political action often start from pain and lead through poverty to powerlessness and stigma. But the sociological explanation of these patterns leads from their most basic causes, which are powerlessness and the culture of the whole society, back to poverty and pain. Both analyses agree that all five elements are inextricably entangled with each other as different aspects of the same larger issue. So we must address all five of these problems if we are to make any progress in solving any of them.

To "target" resources at poverty-stricken groups, without first listening to what they have to say about their own situation – and giving them some power in deciding what shall be done about it – is likely to be fruitless. So is offering to ease their pain with social work and medical care without doing anything about their poverty. This is not just a question of civility – though it is that too. It is also a scientific requirement for discovering truth. When they deal with the excluded, the dominant groups, left to themselves, always get things at least partly wrong.

Conventional approaches to progressive politics which start from liberty, fraternity or equality, or from ideas of rights and citizenship, can now be seen in clearer perspective. I do not reject them, but, taken by themselves, they are weakened by the awkward questions they pose. Why should we adopt one of these

181

values in preference to the others? *Whose* liberties or rights – or whatever – are to be given priority over others'? And how far do we have to go? When can we conclude that we have enough liberty, equality, or whatever? In the approach which I have outlined, these conventional starting points of progressive argument, are not the prime movers, but the implications and consequences of a simpler drive to reduce preventable pain. In countries like Britain it is clear that we must go a long way further towards creating a freer, more comradely and more equal society which guarantees human rights more effectively if we are to make much progress in reducing pain and its attendant evils of poverty, powerlessness and stigma.

The determination to reduce pain, which is the starting point of this system of ideas, is not just an arbitrarily chosen assertion of personal preference. It springs from concerns, widely held in many cultures, which are related in verifiable ways to other values. The choice of this network of related values and observations as reasons for social action is prompted by the circumstances of a particular place and time (Britain today). It provides ways of measuring the problems to be found there, and keeping track of our success or failure in solving them.

But the journey is not infinite. When pain and poverty are no longer concentrated in particular groups but randomly scattered, when they are no longer correlated with each other or with shortened life expectations and unhappiness, and when they are no longer transmitted from one generation to the next, then we should switch our attention to new issues which will become more urgent. Some countries have made a good deal more progress in these directions than our own has.

It is a journey we make. Although it has no final destination, we know at any particular time and place which way we should be heading.

Policy implications

Power relations – which are where the problems of pain begin – are rooted in the economy. If there are masses of unemployed workers at the bottom of the labour market, the less fortunate and the least skilled have no hope of securing the training, the pay and the respect they deserve. Opportunities for everyone to do decent work at a respectable wage must be the prime aim – not only for those squarely in the labour force, but for many others: for pensioners who would prefer more flexible retirement ages, for students who want to work their way through college, for prisoners who instead of sitting locked in their cells could earn money for their families or make restitution to their victims, for mentally handicapped people trying to find a way into the mainstream of society, and for many others now excluded and impoverished on the fringes of society.

To achieve full employment we shall need a programme for national recovery in which all the main interest groups can collaborate. That will include what used to be called an incomes and prices policy, although it will doubtless have to be given a new name. Without that, we shall revert to the "incomes policy" of keeping millions out of work: a policy which keeps a precarious lid on inflation, industrial disputes and social conflict in the short run – over bubbling depths of depression, anger and threatened disorder.

Disputes about differentials have repeatedly destroyed previous compacts of this kind. Thus agreements about the distribution of incomes and the range of earnings which should be tolerated within one organisation or profession provide an essential foundation for any compact that is to last. Countries which have maintained low levels of unemployment and industrial disputes, despite massive industrial restructuring, have usually made "wage solidarity" – bringing about a gradual movement towards greater equality of earnings – a central feature of their policies. The more skilled and better organised workers have foregone some of the increases in pay which their industrial muscle could have won for them because they judged that to be better for the country as a whole. That kind of restraint is not achieved without a lot of argument and education.

In Britain we have not even begun talking about what would be a proper distribution of earnings. Like sex in Victorian times, it is a taboo topic.

Even if workers and employers agree to a more equal distribution of incomes, many of the lower paid workers with several children to care for are likely to be in difficulties. In Britain, these people and their families are, by most measures, the largest group now in poverty. Their wages make too little provision for the dependents they have to support. Thus an adequate level of child benefits, and other forms of family support provided through housing, health and other services, will be an essential component of any policy designed to reduce poverty. The taxes required to finance these services and the ways in which their burdens are distributed among different kinds of people will also form part of the bargain to be struck at national level between workers, employers and the government.

At local level, we shall need new, decentralised forms of administration which break up monopolies, promote competition, and make all services – public, private or voluntary – more accountable to their customers. We shall need more determined initiatives to help people marooned on the margins of the economy back into full-time work – often through publicly funded agencies which they see as their own. They have little reason to trust governments.

These strategies call for very demanding kinds of civic leadership, capable of giving local groups ample scope for independent action, yet providing advice and support when it is needed; capable, too, of insisting that a broader and more far sighted perspective is maintained if local groups engage in destructive competition, or become corrupted. That kind of leadership may be provided mainly by local councillors, but if they lack the powers or the ability for the task, other sources of civic concern (such as the churches in Ireland, North and South) may have to take on the role.

I have stopped short of discussing the international scale of action, except to note that no system for the protection of human rights can be relied on if it is left entirely to national governments to administer it. They will find too many reasons for neglecting our rights. An international court of appeal will be needed, based in countries sharing common interests and common standards of public behaviour. Dedicated defenders of human rights cannot also be dedicated nationalists. There are other reasons, too, for taking the international scale more seriously in future. In an increasingly free-flowing world market, policies about the level and distribution of earnings and social benefits cannot be determined wholly within the frontiers of one nation. The European Communities have made a good start on enlarging and protecting the rights of workers. But they have been less concerned about non-workers. Lone parents, the physically and mentally handicapped, and the long-term unemployed are getting left behind.

These are some of the practical implications of the political philosophy I have proposed. They would be rejected out of hand by many on the Right. But they also help to explain why Britain's Left is in serious disarray. The British trade unions, are belatedly coming to recognise that they need help from the European Community if they are to defend their members' rights against depredations by their employers and their own government; but most of them have been lukewarm or hostile towards all the other proposals listed: an incomes policy, generous policies for family support, and the decentralisation and democratisation of public services.

Already some ominous results of these divided loyalties are to be seen. Perhaps for lack of any conviction that they can put together a programme for national recovery that will work, the Labour leadership seems to be abandoning its commitment to get back to full employment.

Conservative leaders claim to have eliminated major strikes from the economy, but every time it grows strongly enough to give workers greater confidence, industrial conflict comes to the boil again. If British governments come to rely on high rates of unemployment to keep inflation down and industrial disputes under control, we shall have to live permanently with a deeply divided working class, a divided Labour movement, and a large fringe of unemployed or intermittently working people, many of whom have to find illicit ways of getting by. Burglary, the drug traffic, riots and the police force are among the assured growth areas of such an economy.

Reversing these trends will take time and a great deal of hard work. To say that it can be done is true, because other countries have done it. But we cannot simply import institutions from nations whose formative historical experiences have been quite different from our own. Their example can give us the courage to try new approaches, but we shall have to work out our own solutions.

New political issues

It may be objected that this progressive agenda takes no account of the "new" political issues of race, gender, sexual orientation, nationalism and green politics which, collectively, will demand growing attention in the years to come.

The omission does not mean that I underestimate their importance. But it is not accidental. If we do not first make progress towards a fairer, less divided, more equal society we cannot successfully tackle these issues.

The Americans provide a vivid warning of what happens if we continue down the road we are already taking. Abandoning a quite courageous nationwide attempt to reduce poverty, they enabled the luckier and the abler women and ghetto residents to fight for larger shares of the better jobs, the homes in the leafier suburbs, and all the other privileges of their massively affluent, profoundly unequal society. Many succeed. Women are gaining more of the top jobs, and there is now a wealthy, confident, black middle class. But they have left behind in the inner cities a mass of people, black and white – nothing so coherent as an "underclass" – who are far more exploited, poverty stricken and disorganised than their predecessors who lived in the inner city ghettos of the 1960s.

Social justice is also basic in tackling "green" problems. If we allow the poorer countries of the Third World to fall further and further behind in a Devil-take-the-hindmost race for affluence, we cannot expect them to refrain from felling and burning the rain forests, slaughtering the elephants and rhinos, using the cheapest and most polluting fuels and feeding our own societies' demands for heroin and cocaine. They will not accept – why should they? – that they are to be permanently excluded from opportunities which more fortunate countries take for granted.

The same questions have to be put to nationalists. If the devolution of powers to a Scottish assembly passes some of those powers right down the line to people living in places like Easterhouse, Wester Hailes and other deprived neighbourhoods, that could be fruitful. But if it only transfers powers to an assembly dominated by one party and their associated civil servants and lawyers in Edinburgh, few outside that restricted circle will have high hopes of the change.

That does not mean that we must solve every other social problem before turning to the new issues. We should do our best to respond to each problem we encounter. But fairness and justice, in the senses I have set forth here, are fundamental to the way in which we approach all of them.

QUESTIONS

1 If you could by law compel governments to publish each year figures showing the extent to which their countries have succeeded in reducing inequalities in – and the links between – pain and poverty, what kinds of data would you ask for?

2 Taking part in a televised political debate, you say we need principles that would govern the differences in earnings which should be tolerated in any enterprise or profession. Your chairman, with an expression of embarrassment, switches at once to another topic and speaker. How would you respond? What principles would you propose?

3 The arguments of this chapter might suggest that the Labour party or some other progressive movement should set out to represent all the most deprived groups in society. But "rainbow coalitions" of this sort rarely work well. Why? And how would you respond to this dilemma?

4 Which countries seem to have made the best progress towards the objectives summarised in this chapter? Do they have any other common features? If so, what lessons would you learn from them?

5 What kinds of people should be the heroes and heroines of up-to-date myths for progressives? And who would be the villains?

6 "Pain, poverty, powerlessness and stigma" are all dreary things. Can you suggest more positive concepts to capture the imagination? "One nation". "Fair shares for all". These used to be the slogans of the Conservative and Labour parties. They may seem a bit threadbare now; but can we do better?

11 | *Is anybody listening?*

Introduction

Many of those who have read this far and perhaps agree with most of what I have said will wonder whether anybody who is likely to wield power would take these arguments seriously. Could this book be no more than a nostalgia trip? A dwindling echo in the minds of a dwindling generation who still recall the days when the people of many countries were trying to create a world which would offer satisfying work at fair wages for everyone who wanted a job; a good, free health service available to all when they needed it; schools to which all would be happy to send their own children; a secure and decent home for every family at a rent or price they could afford; and at the end of the day a pension scheme in which all would share?

Don't let's romanticise the past. We had not yet achieved all those things. But at least we knew where we were going. Meanwhile, with little more than a ritual grumble, we waited our turn in the Health Service queues; we sent our children to comprehensive schools; we knew that people rarely cheated the social security system because they could easily get jobs that paid them far more money; and because our defence depended on nationwide conscription we believed that our government would have to convince us all of the justice of its cause before getting into another war. We also thought it our duty to pay taxes and local rates which were designed, roughly speaking, to load the costs of extending people's rights upon those who could best bear the burden.

To many younger people today that world must seem as distant as the middle ages. They have been taught that it is their duty to jump the Health Service queues by buying private medical

188

care; to buy their way out of the pension schemes in which we all shared into the best benefits which their own good health and generous tax reliefs will make available; to evade whenever they can the payment of taxes which make no pretence of being fair; to leave complicated things like the country's defence in the hands of experts prepared to contemplate pressing the nuclear buttons; to turn their backs upon the growing numbers of people who are poor, and to pay for the extra police and prisons required to protect us all from those among them who turn nasty.

Meanwhile, through the 1980s, our principal teacher went relentlessly on. "Noone would remember the Good Samaritan if he'd only had good intentions. He had money as well." "There is no such thing as society. There are individual men and women and there are families."

It is important to remember that Mrs Thatcher's governments were elected by about two-fifths of those who voted: roughly the same proportions of the electorate that voted for the previous Conservative leader when he lost the 1974 election. What distinguishes Margaret Thatcher from Edward Heath is not the massive support she secured from the British people but the collapse of coherent opposition. The swing of votes to the Conservatives was in fact quite modest. Most of the British stand, politically, much where they did before. The opposition parties' disastrous loss of Parliamentary seats was largely due to their own divisions, and the mechanics of Britain's electoral system, based on simple majorities in single-member constituencies.

The lesson to be learnt from this story is not that proportional representation, tactical voting or any other piece of political engineering will solve the problems of the Left. It is that until the Left can unite to fashion convincing economic and social policies it will only discredit itself once more if it gains power. And to whom will the voters turn then?

How political changes come about

Profoundly unequal societies – and Britain is clearly one of those – are always apt to run into periods of turbulence when groups which have long been neglected demand a fairer share of the nation's resources. The hold upon power of the society's dominant classes is shaken at these times and a new settlement of major issues

189

emerges, leading to fundamental changes in policies and priorities. Often these periods follow from major wars. (Not the smaller wars conducted by professional soldiers.) These compel the ruling classes to show greater concern for the mass of their people upon whose willingness to remain steadfast through danger and hardship their survival depends. They also give the state, through war-time taxation, a much larger share of the national income, some of which it retains to pay for new social programmes. But war is not the only cause of turbulence. Most of the East European countries have recently embarked on cataclysmic changes without having first to pass through war or violent revolution. Many would dispute the precise dating of these periods in a nation's history; but in Britain most would include in their lists the years immediately following 1832, 1905, 1918 and 1945.

I am not suggesting that nothing changes between these turbulent periods. But many of the changes which do take place amount to new applications of the ideas which gained ascendancy in the course of the previous settlement. Or they may be tentative experiments preparing the way for the next major advance. Thus the Marxist account of social change, which claims that major political developments are brought about by conflict, has a lot of truth in it.

However, the window for change which opens during these critical periods soon closes. Within a couple of years new economic crises and political demands impinge on the government, reducing its freedom of action; and the costs of its first major commitments begin to be felt, making it much harder to find resources for new projects. Thus radical innovations which seemed for a while to be feasible soon become unthinkable again.

Radical incoming governments have little time to find proposals for change which will establish the authority of their regimes. There is no time for research, for controlled experiments or for Royal Commissions. Convincing proposals for action have to be made within months – sometimes within days. These are drawn from the stockpile of ideas for making the world a better place which have been assembled over the previous generation or two by people who experimented with them, researched upon them, and spread them by writing, talking and teaching, and by their own example. William Beveridge's proposals for reforming the social security system, which were legislated almost straight into the statute book by the Attlee Government between 1946 and 1948, are an example of this process. They had been developed by him and many others over a period extending back to before the First World War. The health services, which had been debated in repeated reports over the previous generation, were transformed in much the same way. But postwar housing policies, which had not been exposed to so much debate, amounted to a repetition, with little change, of the prescription worked out between the wars.

The process continues today. Many of the ideas seized upon by Margaret Thatcher and her colleagues after 1979 were formulated by Milton Friedman and Friederich von Hayek a generation earlier. Meanwhile, in countries like Romania, where for a generation any kind of experimental thinking was dangerous, it is peculiarly difficult to make good use of the opportunity now offered for radical change.

People do not give power away willingly. There is always an existing regime – never a clean slate. Its bureaucracies and professions, its more satisfied customers, its political leaders and their policemen defend this system fiercely. Major changes only come about when they *have* to: and that means when previous policies and the regimes responsible for them have been widely discredited, and something better seems to be available. The use which politicians then make of the windows for change opened by social conflict depends on the ideas laboriously formulated, tested and disseminated in previous years. To make the world a better place, a revolution has to build on the foundations laid by reformers who may already be dead. Thus the rational liberal theory that research, experiment and education play important parts in bringing about changes in policy also has a great deal of truth in it.

Within a particular culture we know a good deal about the kinds of people who play key parts in preparing the way for reform. We also know the kinds of organisation which have provided the bases and networks they required. In Britain those tend to be fairly small, unprestigious, interstitial groups, lying between the big power structures. They are in touch with the powerful, but keep their distance from them. They bring together people from various traditions and walks of life. Ideas for reform scarcely ever originate in government departments or in the well established political parties, trade unions, and professional associations. Eccentric individuals – some with a foothold inside these organisations –

play parts in developing these ideas. Then later, as social changes bring them onto the political and professional agendas, all these institutions have to take the ideas up and put their shoulders to the wheel before they can be put into practice effectively.

You cannot write the history of social reform in Britain through the early and middle years of this century without repeatedly encountering the London School of Economics and Political Science, the Fabian Society, and Toynbee Hall – an East End settlement – and people like the Webbs, Richard Tawney, William Beveridge and Clement Attlee who played a part in most of them. You cannot write the history of the previous generation of reformers without repeatedly encountering the idealist philosophers of Oxford around T.H. Green, the Charity Organisation Society, and again Toynbee Hall. And before that it was the evangelical churches; and the utilitarians; and so on, back into history. Well aware of these mechanisms, Conservative groups have taken a great deal of trouble to build equivalent "think tanks" of their own in recent years. The reformers who play a part in shaping important social changes do not always do right. Indeed, what seems "right" in the circumstances of one generation may seem utterly wrong in the next. Thus we now condemn some of the ideas of the most widely revered of these people – ideas such as William Beveridge's on the role of women in the family and the work force, and the implications of that role for social security programmes. Other visions of the future have proved still more profoundly mistaken. The Charity Organisation Society's deeply rooted hostility to the state helped for many years to obstruct urgently needed reforms before the Society was eventually marooned up a backwater of history. Likewise the churches, which played so large a part in building schools, obstructed for two generations the development of an effective nationwide system of education.

"Think tanks", with their élitist reliance on a small band of influential, London-centred academics and political fixers, will not be the best instrument for advancing our understanding of the needs of poverty-stricken groups and the politically powerless. It would be very odd if they were. Excluded groups will have to do that for themselves, with the support of others working "in the field", grappling with practical problems and doing their best to meet urgent human needs in more effective ways. Together they will make a contribution to reforming ideas which will often be more fitting – if less widely recognised in the history books.

Conclusions

These are the conclusions I draw from this brief excursion into history.

In a society as unequal as Britain's, times of turbulence leading to fundamental reappraisals of political priorities, are not over and done with. History has not stopped. Such times will come again, for sure; but in ways that few will foresee and noone can orchestrate: perhaps not even in our own lifetimes. The task of reform is a long distance event – not a sprint. But when the time comes, things move fast: politicians look desperately for responses which offer some hope to their people and confirm their own hold on power.

Meanwhile people in many quarters are working hard to assemble a stockpile of tried and tested ideas to offer governments in such a time of crisis. Not all of them are attractive. Among the most threatening is the scenario, already well rehearsed in Ulster, which brings about the virtual abolition of democratic local government, and the abolition of trial by jury for many offenses. It also brings the army onto the streets to man checkpoints and carry out house searches, backed by an armed police force, and official censorship which bans certain movements from the mass media. All these are waiting to be slotted into place in Britain should the opportunity arise.

Thus turbulence, creating political crises, does not necessarily lead in humane or equalising directions. In democracies during peace time it has often led to fascism or something like it.

The opportunities for change created by turbulence will only lead to good things if good people have worked hard for many years to make that possible by thinking out better ways of running the world, trying their ideas out whenever they get a chance, and teaching other people what they have learnt.

People cannot question the assumptions of the dominant groups in their society all by themselves. To formulate new ways of doing things and set them in motion they need the support of other people who share their perception of the world and help them to challenge the conventional wisdom: a "resistance movement" of some sort. Women have been quite successful in doing this. Black minorities in a white world have found it harder, but not impossible. Many other oppressed groups have yet to gain an effective hearing. They need the tolerance and encouragement

193

which can be offered by an open, plural, secular society – a society that respects every tradition which gives others the freedom to flourish that it claims for itself. They also need practical help from people within the bureaucracies, the political parties and the news media – "subversives" of a sort – who understand the labyrinths of power and show them how to find their way through them. We can all help. And if we don't, we hinder.

What seem bad times for people of a reforming spirit – when hostile forces dominate their world and they find it difficult to imagine that their own small voices will ever gain a hearing – can also be very important times. Most of the published works now quoted in political debate as exercising a seminal influence upon action were written when their authors had no influence upon the powerful, and may indeed have been known only to a few professional colleagues. (Hayek and Friedman, recent gurus of British governments, are no exception.)

Reformers who write books and pamphlets and keep diaries tend to be given more of the credit for bringing about changes than is their due. They often learn the most important lessons they have to offer by observing, and working with, people doing practical things in their field.

The role of central government, too, tends to be overrated. In many fields – education, social work and housing are full of examples – its main task has usually been to persuade the mass of local authorities to do things already pioneered by the most innovative spirits in local government and voluntary movements (often in the teeth of opposition from central Ministries); and to provide the funds which make that possible.

Thus we should neither assume that a change of government will make much difference, nor despair if it fails to do so. What each of us does is important. We do not have to accept the values which oppressive regimes seek to impose on us. Those regimes will not last for ever. But whether they will be succeeded by something better or something worse will depend on all of us.

This book began with a text from Habakkuk who reminds us that we are not the first to find ourselves in a society which seems to have abandoned that quest. It ends with another from T.S. Eliot who teaches us how to behave in such a world.

. . .what there is to conquer
By strength and submission, has already been discovered
Once or twice, or several times, by men whom one cannot hope
To emulate – but there is no competition –
There is only the fight to recover what has been lost
And found and lost again and again: and now, under conditions
That seem unpropitious. But perhaps neither gain nor loss.
For us, there is only the trying. The rest is not our business.

Further reading

These notes provide full references to any source mentioned in this book, and some suggestions about further reading for those who want to explore the issues it deals with. They also record where earlier versions of several chapters in the book appeared. I am grateful to the publishers and editors who allowed me to give my ideas a trial run in their pages.

The notes are arranged under the titles of the chapters to which they refer, and come in the order of the topics in those chapters which they deal with. I have capitalised the main title of each book and written their sub-titles without capitals. The publishers for whom no location is given are all London-based. "HMSO" stands for Her Majesty's Stationery Office, the British government's publisher.

Introduction

The latest evidence of Britain's growing inequality appears in the Fourth Report from the House of Commons' Social Services Committee, *Low Income Statistics*, HMSO, 1990, which appeared too late to be quoted in this book. Evidence about the distribution of earnings – showing a slow but steady trend towards greater inequality at both ends of the range – can be found in *British Labour Statistics Historical Abstract: 1886-1986*, HMSO, 1971, and the Department of Employment's *New Earnings Surveys, 1970-89*. For a clear and comprehensive review of recent patterns in the distribution of British incomes and tax burdens, see John Hills, *Changing Tax*. Child Poverty Action Group (1-5 Bath Street, London EC1), 1988. Some of these sources are quoted in chapter 8.

For countries belonging to the OECD a major research programme called the Luxembourg Income Study is now producing comparable data about incomes. Some of this can be seen in Timothy M. Smeeding, Michael O'Higgins and Lee Rainwater (editors), *Poverty, Inequality and Income Distribution in Comparative Perspective*. The Luxembourg Income Study, Harvester Wheatsheaf, 1990.

One of the best and most readable reviews of recent economic, social and political trends in Britain is Peter Jenkins's *Mrs Thatcher's Revolution*, Pan Books (second edition), 1989.

Nicholas Bosanquet's book, *After the New Right*, Heinemann, 1983, is one of the most thoughtful British reviews of the thinking of the "New" Right. But, writing so soon after Mrs Thatcher's regime began, it is perhaps not surprising that he only begins to sketch out alternative futures for his country. David Marquand, in *The Unprincipled Society*, Jonathan Cape, 1988 – another revealing backward look at the evolution of British society – goes a little further in formulating guidance to a different future. But not much.

However, the attempt to work out alternative, progressive, political principles is beginning. Recent examples include Michael Ignatieff, *The Needs of Strangers*, Chatto and Windus, 1984; Malcolm Wicks, *A Future for All. Do we need the welfare state?*, Penguin Books, 1987; Roy Hattersley, *Choose Freedom. The future for democratic socialism*, Michael Joseph, 1987; Frank Field, *Freedom and Wealth in a Socialist Future*, Constable, revised edition 1987; Nicholas Deakin, *The Politics of Welfare*, Methuen, 1987; and John Baker, *Arguing for Equality*, Verso, 1987. (1987 was obviously a great year for the resistance!) Among more recent works worth attention is Bill Jordan's *The Common Good. Citizenship, morality and self-interest*, Basil Blackwell, 1989.

The Churches have also made a growing contribution in recent years. The most widely discussed of these has been the Report of the Archbishop of Canterbury's Commission on Urban Priority Areas, *Faith in the City. A call for action by Church and nation*, Church House Publishing, 1985. The Church of Scotland has contributed too. See, for example, *Just Sharing. A Christian approach to the distribution of wealth, income and benefits*, edited by Duncan Forrester and Danus Skene, Epworth Press, 1988.

Meanwhile, some of the older books are still well worth reading. See, for example, Richard Tawney's *The Acquisitive*

Society, reissued by Wheatsheaf Books, 1982, and *Equality*, reissued by Allen and Unwin, 1965; also E.P. Thompson, *The Making of the English Working Class*, Penguin Books, revised edition, 1968; and Steven Lukes, *Power: a radical view*, Macmillan, 1974

The most widely quoted contributions to right wing political thinking are: Milton Friedman and Rose Friedman, *Capitalism and Freedom*, University of Chicago Press, 1962, and Friedrich A. Hayek, *The Constitution of Liberty*, Routledge and Kegan Paul, 1960. More local views can be found in Keith Joseph's collected speeches: *Stranded on the Middle Ground? Reflections on circumstances and policies*, Centre for Policy Studies (Wilfred Street, London SW1) 1976, and *Reversing the Trend – a critical reappraisal of Conservative economic and social policies*, Barry Rose, 1975. See also Digby Anderson (editor), *The Kindness That Kills*, Society for the Promotion of Christian Knowledge, 1984.

An American contribution to this sort of literature which has been widely quoted is Charles Murray, *Losing Ground: American social policy 1950-1980*, New York, Basic Books, 1984. For a reply to it, see Fred Block and others, *The Mean Season. The attack on the welfare state*, New York, Pantheon Books, 1987.

1. Seeing, saying and doing

One of the best reports on homeless individuals in Britain is *Single and Homeless* by Madeline Drake, Maureen O'Brien and Tony Biebuyck, published by the Department of the Environment through HMSO in 1981. For accounts of Glasgow's situation and experience, see the Annual Reports produced by the Glasgow Council for the Single Homeless (Second floor, 400 Argyle Street, Glasgow G2 7BG) and their special studies: *Homeless Men Speak for Themselves* (1981), *Homeless Women in Glasgow* (1983), *Rehousing Hostel Residents* (1985), *Turning Points: A strategy on single homelessness in Glasgow* (1989), *Single Homelessness and Housing Need in Glasgow* (1990). See also a chapter by Hamish Allan and Joe Evaskitas in *The Housing Service of the Future*, edited by David Donnison and Duncan Maclennan, Longmans, 1991.

For a summary of the situation among young people in London, see Alex Cosgrave, *Young and Homeless in London*, Housing Services Agency (3 Caledonian Road, London, N1 9DX), 1988.

My brief discussion of the ways in which people interpret what they perceive cannot do justice to a very complicated topic. Among the more helpful works on this subject by philosophers are: Jonathan Dancy (editor), *Perceptual Knowledge*, Oxford University Press, 1988 – see particularly the chapters by F. Dretske (8, "Sensation and Perception") and P.F. Strawson (5, "Perception and its Objects"). See also A.J. Ayer, *The Central Questions of Philosophy*, Weidenfeld and Nicolson, 1973 (chapters 4 and 5).

Philosophers rarely draw on the work of "brain scientists" who have actually tried to find out what goes on in our heads. An exception is the very interesting study carried out in partnership by Karl Popper and John Eccles, *The Self and its Brain*, Routledge and Kegan Paul, 1977 – rarely mentioned by mainstream philosophers.

Many will find that John Berger's illustrated book about art, *Ways of Seeing*, Penguin, 1972, teaches them more about perception than anything the philosophers have written. Joseph Campbell, in *Myths to Live By*, Paladin, 1985, quotes (on pages 211-12) revealing passages from Aldous Huxley and C.D. Broad.

For an account of homelessness in North America, see Michael Dear and Jennifer R. Wolch, *Landscapes of Despair: from deinstitutionalisation to homelessness*, Oxford Polity and Basil Blackwell, Oxford, 1987. Maureen Mercer provides an interesting comparison of the very different policies towards homeless people followed in Glasgow and Boston in *Policy and Provision for the Single Homeless in Glasgow and Boston*, M. Phil. Dissertation, Department of Town and Regional Planning, University of Glasgow, 1985. Now held at The Planning Centre, University of Strathclyde, Glasgow.

For a study of the political uses of language, see Max Atkinson, *Our Masters' Voices. The language and body language of politics*, Methuen, 1984. For a revealing analysis of "structures of meaning" and their implications for policy making, see Peter Marris, *Community Planning and Conceptions of Change*, Routledge and Kegan Paul, 1982 – particularly chapter 1.

For a study comparing the ways in which the "industries" of the "welfare state" have developed in different western countries, see Harold Wilensky, *The Welfare State and Equality: structural and ideological roots of public expenditures*, University of California Press, 1975.

An earlier version of this chapter appeared as "Poverty, power and stigma: the case of the single homeless", in Bengt Turner, et al. (editors), *Between State and Market: housing in the post-industrial era*, Stockholm, Almqvist and Wiksell, 1987.

2. Pain, poverty and power

For discussions of the vulnerability of the poor to economic and social changes, and the ways in which they pay, through their insecurity, for the advances which benefit other people, see Peter Marris, *Community Planning and Conceptions of Change*, Routledge and Kegan Paul, 1982; pages 27-30, and Richard Titmuss, *Social Policy: An introduction*, Allen and Unwin, 1974, chapter 5.

My discussion of the meaning and measurement of poverty draws on the following sources. Peter Townsend, *Poverty in the United Kingdom. A survey of household resources and standards of living*, Penguin Books, 1979; Joanna Mack and Stewart Lansley, *Poor Britain*, Allen and Unwin, 1985; Alwyn Smith and Bobbie Jacobson (editors), *The Nation's Health*, King Edward's Hospital Fund For London, 1988; Ruut Veenhoven, *Conditions of Happiness*, D. Reidel Publishing, Dordrecht, 1984; Ray Pahl, *Divisions of Labour*, Basil Blackwell, Oxford, 1984. Michaela Benzeval, *Back to Black*, King's Fund Institute (undated paper); and David Piachaud, "Poverty in Britain 1899 to 1983", *Journal of Social Policy*, Volume 17, 3, pages 335-50, 1988.

The literature on inequalities in health is now extensive. These are some of the best recent sources. Richard Wilkinson, "Class Mortality Differentials, Income Distribution and Trends in Poverty 1921-1981", *Journal of Social Policy*, Vol. 18, pages 307-6, 1989; Julian le Grand, David Winter and Frances Woolley, "The National Health Service: Safe in Whose Hands?", chapter 4 of *The State of Welfare. The welfare state in Britain since 1974*, John Hills (editor), Oxford University Press, 1990; Peter Townsend and Nick Davidson, *Inequalities in Health: the Black Report*, Penguin, 1982. M. Whitehead, *The Health Divide: Inequalities in health in the 1980s*, London, The Health Education Council, 1987. See also *The Nation's Health*, mentioned above.

Health inequalities appear in every country and do not closely match other kinds of inequality now present in these places – which is a reminder that many other factors, reaching back over the lifetimes of the people now nearing the end of their lives, play a part in shaping these patterns. See John Fox (editor), *Health*

Inequalities in European Countries, Gower, 1989 – particularly chapter 4 by Julian le Grand, "An International Comparison of Distributions of Ages-at-Death".

The Glasgow study of travel to hospitals and surgeries was made by Isobel M.L. Robertson and reported in "Access to the Health Services", chapter 9 of David Donnison and Alan Middleton (editors), *Regenerating the Inner City. Glasgow's experience*, Routledge, 1987.

For a contrary view to my own, see Keith Joseph and Jonathan Sumption, *Equality*, John Murray, 1979.

For a more carefully reasoned criticism of the relative, egalitarian definition of poverty, see Stein Ringen, *The Possibility of Politics*, Oxford University Press, Oxford, 1987. He summarised his criticisms in an article in "Direct and Indirect Measures of Poverty", *The Journal of Social Policy*, Vol.17, No.3, pages 351-66, 1988. I replied in the following pages: "Defining and Measuring Poverty. A Reply to Stein Ringen", (pages 367-74). My response was, in effect, an early draft of the argument presented in this chapter.

For an argument formulated by economists which sets out from a different starting point from my own but arrives at rather similar conclusions, see G.W. Lewis and D.T. Ulph, "Poverty, Inequality and Welfare", *The Economic Journal*, 98, pages 117-31, 1988. They quote another very thoughtful work by an economist: Amartya Sen, *The Standard of Living*, Cambridge University Press, 1987.

3. By what authority?

A.J.Ayer, *Freedom and Morality and Other Essays*, Oxford, Clarendon Press, 1984, page 46.

For an original and revealing discussion by an economist of "tastes" and how they evolve, see Albert Hirschman, *Shifting Involvements. Private interest and public action*, Princeton University Press, 1982 and Basil Blackwell (Oxford), 1985. His colleagues rarely refer to it.

David Sheppard spoke up for the unemployed (among others) in *Bias to the Poor* (Hodder and Stoughton, 1983), and was attacked by Digby Anderson for doing so in *The Kindness That Kills*, Society for the Promotion of Christian Knowledge, 1984, page 75.

Further reading

Keith Joseph and Jonathan Sumption, *Equality*, John Murray, page 19.

Rhodes Boyson, *Down With the Poor*, Churchill Press, 1971, page 5 – quoted by Joanna Mack and Stewart Lansley in *Poor Britain*, Allen and Unwin, 1985, page 227.

John Rawls, *A Theory of Justice*, Oxford, Clarendon Press, 1972 – see pages 302-3 for my quotations. For a totally different approach to political philosophy and the tasks of politics, see Michael Oakeshott, *Rationalism in Politics and Other Essays*, Methuen, 1962. His most frequently quoted statement on the subject comes on page 127.

Robert Nozick, *Anarchy, State and Utopia*, Oxford, Basil Blackwell, 1974. My quotes come from pages 153, 155, 160 and 168.

Ted Honderich, *Violence for Equality. Inquiries in political philosophy*, Penguin, 1980, pages 55 and 56.

Robert Nisbet, "The Pursuit of Equality", chapter 4 in William Letwin (editor) *Against Equality. Readings on economic and social policy*, Macmillan, 1983, page 133.

Albert Weale, *Political Theory and Social Policy*, Macmillan, 1983, pages vii, 38, 43, 45, 180, 197.

My ideas about social groups and the ways in which our values grow out of their changing practices owe a great deal to Alasdair MacIntyre, *After Virtue: a study in moral theory*, Duckworth, 1981 – particularly chapters, 5, 6, 14 and 15.

Thomas S. Kuhn's *The Structure of Scientific Revolutions* (second edition, Chicago University Press, 1970) and J.L. Mackie's *Ethics: Inventing right and wrong*, (Penguin, 1977) are two other very helpful books on these issues.

Stein Ringen, *The Possibility of Politics*, Oxford University Press, 1987.

For more general discussions of moral philosophy, see R.M. Hare, *Moral Thinking. Its levels, method and point*, Oxford University Press, 1981; Philippa Foot (editor), *Theories of Ethics*, Oxford University Press, 1967; and (for me the most helpful) Bernard Williams, *Ethics and the Limits of Philosophy*, Fontana, 1985.

An earlier draft of much of the argument in this chapter appeared in *Reason, Passion and Politics*, the 1987 Ian Gulland Memorial Lecture, Goldsmith's College, University of London.

4. Rights, needs and duties

N. Gangulee (editor) *Giuseppi Mazzini, Selected Writings*, Glasgow, Lindsay Drummond, 1945: pages 151, 161, 163 and 164 – italics in the original.
Public Schools Commission, First Report, HMSO, 1968, page 59.
Isaiah Berlin, *Four Essays on Liberty*, Oxford University Press, 1969, page 166.

For statements of contrasting philosophies about rights, see Jeremy Waldron (editor) *Theories of Rights*, Oxford University Press, 1984; Ronald Dworkin, *Taking Rights Seriously*, Duckworth, 1977; Tom Campbell, *The Left and Rights. A conceptual analysis of the idea of socialist rights*, Routledge and Kegan Paul, 1983.

For a socialist version of the negative view of freedom, see Keith Dixon, *Freedom and Equality. The moral basis of democratic socialism*, Routledge and Kegan Paul, 1986. For a contrasting socialist version of the positive view, see Roy Hattersley, *Choose Freedom. The future for democratic socialism*, Michael Joseph, 1987.

For evidence about racially motivated attacks on people, see Home Office, *Racial Attacks. Report of a Home Office Study*, HMSO, 1981; Ashok Bhat, Roy Carr-Hill and Sushel Ohri, *Britain's Black Population* (second edition), Gower, 1988, chapter 4; and Colin Brown, *Black and White Britain: the Third P.S.I. Survey*, Policy Studies Institute and Heinemann, 1984.

Central Advisory Council for Education (England), *Children and Their Primary Schools*, HMSO, 1967, Vol. II, pages 121-23.

For comparative data on the percentages of children and young people in schools in different countries, see UNESCO, *Statistical Yearbooks*.

For evidence about early leavers, see Roma Morton-Williams and Stewart Finch, *Young School Leavers: Schools Council Enquiry I*, HMSO, 1968 (page 219, for example).

For discussions of the patterns and causes of educational disadvantage, see C. Jencks and others, *Inequality: a reassessment of the effect of family and schooling in America*, Allen Lane, 1973. For studies of the differing British patterns, see Peter Wedge and Hilary Prosser, *Born to Fail?*, Arrow Books, 1973; Michael Rutter and Nicola Madge, *Cycles of Disadvantage. A review of research*, Heinemann, 1976 ; A.H. Halsey, A.F. Heath and J.M. Ridge, *Origins and Destinations: Family, class and education in modern*

Further reading

Britain, Oxford University Press, 1980; and Jo Mortimore and Tessa Blackstone, *Disadvantage and Education*, Heinemann, 1982. For a perceptive analysis of the way in which the distribution of incomes is affected by restrictions on entry to occupations imposed by powerful groups, see Patricia Apps, *A Theory of Inequality and Taxation*, Cambridge University Press, 1981.

Jeff Henderson and Valerie Karn, *Race, Class and State Housing: inequality and the allocation of state housing in Britain*, Aldershot, Gower, 1987.

For a study tracing the recurring appearance of new concepts and terms to describe poor and excluded people, see John MacNicol, "In Pursuit of the Underclass", *Journal of Social Policy*, Vol. 16, 3, 1987, pages 293-318.

For an analysis of the circumstances which tend to strengthen or to weaken demands for rights, see Mancur Olson, *The Logic of Collective Action*, Harvard University Press, 1965 and 1971.

J.A.M. Cobbah discusses African traditions of rights and duties in "African Values and the Human Rights Debate: an African Perspective", *Human Rights Quarterly*, Vol. 9, 1987, pages 309-31.

For an interesting introduction to the origins of law, see Simon Roberts, *Order and Dispute. An introduction to legal anthropology*, Penguin Books, 1979.

For an international perspective on human rights, see Louis Henkin, *The Rights of Man Today*, Stevens,1979.

For summaries of the initiatives taken by the European Communities on human rights, see Commission of the European Communities, *Community Charter of the Fundamental Social Rights of Workers, 1989*; and *Communication from the Commission Concerning its Action Programme Relating to the Implementation of the Community Charter of Basic Social Rights for Workers, 1989*, Brussels and Luxembourg. Note that the rights which most concern the EEC are those of "workers". Little is said about the rights of people who are unable to get paid work. For a clear, brief discussion of the opportunities and the dangers arising from closer integration within Europe, see Michael Barratt Brown, *Europe 1992*, European Labour Forum Pamphlet No. 3, Bertrand Russell House, Gamble Street, Nottingham NG7 4ET.

Michael Ignatieff provides a vivid explanation of the irrelevance of purely individualistic rights talk which is not based on a strong, supportive community. See *The Needs of Strangers*,

Chatto and Windus, 1984 (pages 40-53).

An earlier version of this chapter appeared as "Rethinking Rights Talk", a chapter in Lionel Orchard and Robert Dare, *Markets, Morals and Public Policy*, Adelaide, Federation Press, 1989 (pages 219-231).

5. Progressive directions

For a revealing comparison of the role of the state in different advanced capitalist economies, see David Marquand, *The Unprincipled Society*, Fontana, 1988 – chapter 4.

For a discussion of the whole idea of economic growth – a fairly new aspiration in the world's history, still very crudely interpreted – see H.W. Arndt, *The Rise and Fall of Economic Growth. A study in contemporary thought*, Longman Cheshire, Melbourne, 1978.

G.C. Macauley (editor), *The Chronicles of Froissart*, Macmillan, 1895, page 251. Jean-Jacques Rousseau, *The Social Contract* (1762), Dent (Everyman edition), 1913, page 42.

Friedrich Engels, *Anti-Dühring*, Foreign Languages Publishing House, Moscow, 1954, page 149.

Richard Tawney, *Equality*, Allen and Unwin, 1931, page 41.

6. People first

For one of the earliest discussions of the armed forces' need to adopt a "community-based" approach to its work – a book provoking great controversy when it first appeared – see Frank Kitson, *Low Intensity Operations*, Faber and Faber, 1971.

A glimpse of the Labour Party's attempts to rebuild its links with communities can be seen in David Blunkett and C. Green, *Building From the Bottom: the Sheffield Experience*, Fabian Society Pamphlet No. 491, 1983.

For a discussion of the privatisation alternative, see Julian le Grand and Ray Robinson (editors), *Privatisation and the Welfare State*, Allen and Unwin, 1984.

Lord Scarman, *The Brixton Disorders, 10-12 April, 1981: Report of an Inquiry*, Cmnd. 8427, HMSO, 1981.

For information about self-help groups in the health field, see S.Lock, "Self-Help Groups: the Fourth Estate in Medicine?", *British Medical Journal*, No. 293, 20-27 December, 1986, pages 1596-1600.

For a discussion, within a religious context, of many of the issues explored in this chapter, see Rosemary Radford Ruether, *Women-Church*, New York, Harper and Row, 1985 – for example, on pages 22-3, 36, and 75-6.

For more general ideas, derived from many countries, about issues discussed here, see Manuel Castells, *The City and the Grassroots*, Edward Arnold, 1983.

An earlier draft of this chapter appears as "Social Policy: the Community-Based Approach", chapter 12 of Martin Bulmer, Jane Lewis and David Piachaud (editors), *The Goals of Social Policy*, Unwin Hyman, 1989.

7. The civic agenda

For an analysis of the differences in educational attainment of children in different towns, see David Donnison with Paul Soto, *The Good City. A study of urban development and policy in Britain*, Heinemann, 1980, chapter 11.

For a review of research on many of the biggest British cities, and a discussion of policies for the regeneration of failing urban economies, see Peter Hall, *The Inner City in Context*, Heinemann, 1981 and Victor A. Hausner (editor), *Urban Economic Change*, Oxford University Press, 1987.

The latest official analysis of British programmes for creating or preserving jobs in declining areas is Ivan Turok and Urlan Wannop, *Targeting Urban Employment Initiatives*, Department of the Environment, HMSO, 1990. For an independent evaluation see G.C. Cameron, "First Steps in Urban Policy Evaluation in the United Kingdom", *Urban Studies*, vol. 27, no. 4, 1990; pages 475-95.

John Myerscough, in *The Economic Importance of the Arts in Britain*, (Policy Studies Institute, 100 Park Village East, London NW1 3SR, Research Report 672, 1988) examines the local economic impact of investment in the arts, and reaches broadly optimistic conclusions (eg. pages 148-50).

For a discussion of business ethics which gives a central place

Further reading

to the responsibilities of enterprise managers to contribute to the welfare of the communities in which they operate, and stresses the benefits they gain from doing so, see Sheena Carmichael and John Drummond, *Good Business. A guide to corporate responsibility and business ethics*, Century Hutchinson, 1989.

Michael Parkinson gives a vivid account of the things which can go wrong when local civic leadership disintegrates in *Liverpool on the Brink. One city's struggle against government cuts*, Policy Journals, Hermitage, 1985. He makes it clear that responsibility for this disintegration must be shared between the central government and all parties at the local level.

Recurring glimpses of the impact of defence expenditures on the economy of a region can be seen in Martin Boddy, John Lovering and Keith Bassett, *Sunbelt City? A study of economic change in Britain's M4 growth corridor*, Oxford University Press, 1986.

For a good account of the guiding role taken by the Swedish state in a successful but still essentially capitalist economy, see Peter Dickens and others, *Housing, States and Localities*, Methuen, 1985, chapters 2-5.

The "equality" of British towns is analysed and discussed in David Donnison with Paul Soto, *The Good City*, Heinemann, 1980. Other parts of my argument were first presented in the final chapter of David Donnison and Alan Middleton (editors), *Regenerating the Inner City. Glasgow's experience*, Routledge, 1987

8. The national agenda

There is a shelf full of books about the experience of unemployment, reaching back to the 1930s and E. Wight Bakke's classic, *The Unemployed Man*, Nisbet, 1933. The more recent works include: Brian Showler and Adrian Sinfield (editors), *The Workless State: Studies in unemployment*, Martin Robertson, Oxford, 1981; and David Taylor, "Living with Unemployment", chapter 8 in Alan and Carolyn Walker (editors), *The Growing Divide. A social audit, 1979-1987*, Child Poverty Action Group, 1987. They trace the effects of unemployment on health and the impact on statistics of the unemployed of recent changes in official definitions. For a cautiously cool analysis of these issues, see Jon Stern, *Unemployment and its Impact on Morbidity and Mortality*, Centre for Labour

207

Economics, London School of Economics (Houghton St, Aldwych, London WC2) Discussion Paper 93, 1981. For an explanation of the difficulties of measuring the numbers of people out of work, see David Gow in the *Guardian*, 14 May, 1987.

British attitudes towards different vulnerable groups and the services on which they depend are monitored in *British Social Attitudes*, a series of reports edited by Roger Jowell and others and published by Gower for "Social and Community Planning Research". The sixth of these is a special international report comparing Britain with other western countries (Gower, 1989). The 1986 report is particularly helpful.

A comparison of attitudes to poverty in the twelve countries of the European Community can be found in *Eurobarometer. The perception of poverty in Europe in 1989*, Commission of the European Communities, March 1990.

A continuous stream of clear and easily readable information about trends in employment and unemployment and policies affecting both is produced by the Employment Institute, Southbank House, Black Prince Road, London SE1 7SJ. For the most thorough recent analysis see G.D.N. Worswick, *Unemployment: a problem of policy*, Cambridge University Press, 1991.

For an American analysis of urban poverty which clearly demonstrates why those who deplore it must place the reduction of unemployment at the top of their policy agendas, see William Julius Wilson, *The Truly Disadvantaged. The inner city, the underclass and public policy*, Chicago University Press, 1987.

Organisation for European Economic Co-operation, 2 Andre Pascal, 75775, Paris, France.

John Hills, *Changing Tax*, Child Poverty Action Group, 1988.

Henry Phelps Brown, *The Inequality of Pay*, Oxford University Press, 1977, is the classic text on the distribution of earnings. He is pessimistic about the scope for modifying these patterns.

The Swedish example has been referred to with some enthusiasm several times in this book. A thoughtful comparison of the ways in which political ideas have developed in Britain and Sweden can be found in Richard Scase, *Social Democracy in Capitalist Society: working class politics in Britain and Sweden*, Croom Helm, 1977. Arnold J. Heidenheimer, Hugh Heclo and Carolyn Teich Adams provide an international comparison of policies and policy making which includes Sweden in *Comparative Public Policy. The politics of social choice in Europe and America*, Macmillan, 1976.

For a comparison of British and Swedish housing policy and practice, see Peter Dickens and others, *Housing, States and Localities*, Methuen, 1985.

A hostile account of the Swedish regime can be found in Roland Huntford, *The New Totalitarians*, Allen Lane, The Penguin Press, 1971. Huntford believes the Swedes are following the path foreseen by Aldous Huxley in *Brave New World*. I do not recognise the picture he paints; but I may have been lucky in my Swedish friends.

For a study of the sources from which students learn, showing the help they get from fellow students, see Peter Marris, *The Experience of Higher Education*, Routledge and Kegan Paul, 1964.

Department of Employment, *New Earnings Survey, 1970-1989*. *British Labour Statistics: Historical Abstract: 1886-1968*, HMSO, 1971. *The Government's Expenditure Plans, 1989*, HMSO, 1989.

For a discussion of the whole question of family benefits and child support, see Joan C. Brown, *The Future of Family Income Support*, Policy Studies Institute (100 Park Village East, London NW1 3SR) Research Report No. 670; and Melanie Henwood and Malcolm Wicks, *Benefit or Burden? The objectives and impact of child support*, Family Policy Studies Centre, 1986. See also David Piachaud, *Round About Fifty Hours a Week: the time costs of children*, Child Poverty Action Group, 1984.

The book I quoted by Stein Ringen is *The Possibility of Politics*, Oxford University Press, 1987.

For a revealing analysis of the fate of those who live in the American ghettos, see William Julius Wilson, *The Truly Disadvantaged. The inner city, the underclass and public policy*, University of Chicago Press, 1987.

My explanation of the redistributive effects of child benefit and the taxation which pays for it owes a great deal to Peter Kellner (writing in the *Independent*, 21 November 1988).

For an account of growing inequalities in Britain and the contribution made to these trends by government policies, see Alan Walker and Carolyn Walker (editors), *The Growing Divide. A social audit, 1979-1987*, Child Poverty Action Group, 1987; and Thomas Stark, *A New A-Z of Income and Wealth. Britain in the 1980s*, Fabian Society (11 Dartmouth Street, London SW1H 9BN) 1988.

The best and latest British assessment of the impact made on the "welfare state" by the changes introduced in recent years is *The*

Further reading

State of Welfare, edited by John Hills, Oxford University Press, 1990. See the final chapter, by Julian le Grand, for a summary of their conclusions. See also Julian le Grand and David Winter, "The Middle Classes and the Welfare State Under Conservative and Labour Governments", *Journal of Public Policy*, 6, 1989, pages 399-430.

9. A service for people

These are some of the more recent and helpful books about British housing problems and housing policies.

Michael Ball, Michael Harloe and Martens Maartje, *Housing and Social Change in Europe and the USA*, Routledge, 1988.

Centre for Housing Research, *The Nature and Effectiveness of Housing Management in England*, HMSO, 1989.

David Donnison and Duncan Maclennan (editors), *The Housing Service of the Future*, Longman, 1991.

Patrick Dunleavy, *The Politics of Mass Housing in Britain, 1945-1975. A study of corporate power, and professional influence in the welfare state*, Oxford University Press, 1981.

Jeff Henderson and Valerie Karn, *Race, Class and State Housing: Inequality and the allocation of public housing in Britain*, Gower, 1987.

Alan E. Holmans, *Housing Policy in Britain*, Croom Helm, 1987.

Alan Murie, *Housing Inequality and Deprivation*, Heinemann, 1983.

The National Federation of Housing Associations, *Inquiry Into British Housing, Report, 1985* – often known as the *Duke of Edinburgh's Inquiry*.

Anne Power, *Property Before People. The management of twentieth century council housing*, Allen and Unwin, 1987.

10. Conclusions

This chapter reviews and summarises the argument of the whole book. It draws on few new sources. The book, briefly mentioned, by Aneurin Bevan is *In Place of Fear*, Heinemann, 1952.

Karl Marx and Frederick Engels wrote perceptively about the way in which a society's dominant groups "own" its ideas. See *The German Ideology*, edited by C.J. Arthur, Lawrence and Wishart, 1970, pages 64-65.

11. Is anybody listening?

It is difficult to pick books which throw light on the ways in which changes in the political climate and in public policy come about. Any good study of political history and many good novels have something to offer. Along with other books already mentioned, these are some of the contributions by social scientists which I have found helpful. There are many more.

T.H. Marshall, *Citizenship and Social Class, and Other Essays*, Cambridge University Press, 1950.

David Easton, *A Framework for Political Analysis*, Prentice-Hall, 1965.

Anthony Downs, *An Economic Theory of Democracy*, Harper, 1957.

Albert O. Hirschman, *Exit, Voice, and Loyalty*, Harvard University Press, 1970.

Karl Marx and Frederick Engels, *The German Ideology*, Lawrence and Wishart, 1965.

Ralf Dahrendorf, *Essays in the Theory of Society*, Routledge and Kegan Paul, 1968.

Phoebe Hall, Hilary Land, Roy Parker and Adrian Webb, *Change, Choice and Conflict in Social Policy*, Heinemann, 1975.

Manuel Castells, *The City and the Grassroots*, Edward Arnold, 1983.

Paul Barker (editor), *Founders of the Welfare State*, Heinemann, 1984 – in which my own concluding chapter is an early draft of the final chapter of this book.

The quotation from T.S. Eliot comes from *Four Quartets*, Faber and Faber, 1944, page 22.

Index